TEEN PROBLEMS AND HOW ADULTS CAN HELP SOLVE THEM

TEEN PROBLEMS AND HOW ADULTS CAN HELP SOLVE THEM

STEPHEN ABRAMOWITZ

TEEN PROBLEMS AND HOW ADULTS CAN HELP SOLVE THEM

iUniverse books may be ordered through booksellers or by contacting:

iUniverse
1663 Liberty Drive
Bloomington, IN 47403
www.iuniverse.com
844-349-9409

Because of the dynamic nature of the Internet, any web addresses or links contained in this book may have changed since publication and may no longer be valid. The views expressed in this work are solely those of the author and do not necessarily reflect the views of the publisher, and the publisher hereby disclaims any responsibility for them.

Any people depicted in stock imagery provided by Getty Images are models, and such images are being used for illustrative purposes only.
Certain stock imagery © Getty Images.

ISBN: 978-1-6632-6726-9 (sc)
ISBN: 978-1-6632-6727-6 (e)

Library of Congress Control Number: 2024920773

Print information available on the last page.

iUniverse rev. date: 09/24/2024

Contents

Introduction

Young teens have problems. In fact, they have lots of problems. Many people simplify the issues that affect teens by separating them into two categories, namely, physical and emotional, but doing this merely avoids the complexity. Young people must deal with challenging matters such as learning difficulties, physical growth, identity, relationships, drugs, familial problems, and consequences of decisions they make. Being a teen has become one of the toughest jobs ever. I often wonder how any teen can grow up to become a productive member of society.

Teen Problems and How Adults Can Help Solve Them is designed to help students in middle school and high school deal with problems they face on an everyday basis. It is designed to be a useful tool for parents, teachers, and/or health professionals wishing to help a child through a life crisis. The lessons are not designed to replace the guidance of responsible parents but are meant as opinions to share with your child's peers, teachers, and health professionals. We all know the effects of negative peer pressure on our children. Through these discussions, a child can be similarly affected, but in a positive way.

The topics are common to problems at school, problems at home, problems that arise while socializing, and even problems that occur when trying to deal with internal issues. These are necessary to discuss because parents, health professionals, and teachers either are unable to help children for logistical reasons or are unaware of the peer pressures that students face. *Teen Problems and How Adults Can Help Solve Them* contains forty discussions of issues that are most common to young teens trying to navigate their world.

Technology has created a new world for our students, with great benefits. However, it has also created negative effects that are more intense than any problems the parents of today's teens ever had to deal with. As you read this, NASA is planning to send astronauts to Mars, companies are planning to test flying cars, and a child somewhere is riding a roller coaster by connecting a wire from his iPhone to a helmet. I recently read a magazine article describing yet another fourteen-year-old girl who committed suicide after being bullied by classmates. Unfortunately, her parents had no idea that she was in trouble. We've all read such stories of preteens or teens in trouble whose parents were clueless.

The key to the program outlined herein is face-to-face communication, an art that is quickly becoming obsolete. How many times have you gone to a restaurant for a meal and found your children or those at a neighboring table with their eyes buried somewhere in their laps? Instead of talking, despite the fact that they are three feet away from each other, your children are texting each other or sending emails to friends. In schools where cell phones are not banned, teachers are plagued with the never-ending problem of texting. Still, we must accept the fact that children can reach out to a variety of people instantly. This saves time and effort, and allows for quick and multiple responses.

Communication possibilities and types have been expanded by technology. Students, who now have access to computers, tablets, and mobile phones, can use these devices to find virtually anything they are curious about. This reduces the need to ask parents, teachers, and health professionals for help and for answers to questions that were previously reserved for these individuals. In addition, a child with a tablet not only obtains more information than a parent can give but also may find that the information found online is sometimes superior to that provided by an adult.

My friend told me a beautiful story about his son who is between one and two years old. While sitting at the dinner table, his son counted to ten flawlessly. The child was also able to yell out words he saw on the television screen. Upon investigation, my friend realized that his son was turning on his iPad and maneuvering to educational sites prompted by his favorite TV puppets. By clicking on the links to the videos, the son was teaching himself how to count and read words.

Teachers have realized that they are able to disseminate huge amounts of information by giving assignments involving internet research. Even a doctor's diagnosis and prescriptions can be checked online, making the need for questions unnecessary. The result is that the need to talk to others is greatly reduced. One of the consequences of the immediate gratification obtained by solving problems on their own is that our students appear to be immature in their dealings with peers and adults. This leads to conflicts in the upper grades and later, in the workplace.

What does this new form of communication mean for our students in school? They no longer have to work in groups because they all have the same information at their fingertips. Teachers must adjust to this new situation and concentrate more on guiding students toward information and less on actually feeding it to them.

One negative aspect of the change to technological communications is social media use. Although these new methods greatly enhance knowledge and keep people in touch with one another, they can become platforms for many types of abuse. Because pupils no longer need to talk face-to-face, they feel free and even encouraged to gossip and tell tales on one another. Recipients can form opinions about others without allowing the subject a face-to-face conversation in defense of his or her own actions.

The discussions outlined in *Teen Problems and How Adults Can Help Solve Them*, however, must be conducted without malice and in such a way as to avoid confrontation. The chosen method of communication for delivering the messages is role-playing. If topics cannot be discussed as presented, then students will be given prepared scripts and will act out situations that are relevant to teens today.

Before beginning any lessons, it is critical for the leader[1] to explain that no student should take any topic personally and that the role-players are presenting a concept that may apply to anyone or to no one. Make a comparison to films, emphasizing that actors represent other people

---

[1] The introduction to *Teen Problems and How Adults Can Help Solve Them* provides instructions and how-tos mostly for teachers, and occasionally for health professionals or parents. And indeed, the leader of the lessons of this curriculum may be a teacher, a health professional, a parent, a friend, or even another student. But note that not all components of each topic discussed are applicable for each type of leader. For example, a parent instructing a child at home would not have the ability, obviously, to draw on a classroom full of students for discussion and input. It is left to the reader to tailor the individual lessons to the intended audience, taking into account his or her (as the leader) circumstances and available resources for leading units of this curriculum. Also, the reader will have to make adjustments—for example, when this text uses *student* but really the one being instructed is the leader's child or patient.

STEPHEN ABRAMOWITZ

and that the characters they play usually have nothing to do with their lives or families. It might be wise for leaders to prepare students by making up unrelated scripts so as to give them practice interacting with others in nonthreatening situations.

Although *Teen Problems and How Adults Can Help Solve Them* is aimed at older students and focuses on the problems inherent to their lives, it also deals with many similar problems that arise in the younger grades. The goals are the same: keep students safe, build their self-esteem, and teach them to problem-solve. The method to success is communication, and the way to communicate is through face-to-face discussion.

The sessions you are about to conduct are based on problems that teens must deal with in their schools and in their everyday lives. Students must be made aware that one out of every seven adults in the country suffers from some form of addiction. They must be made aware that one out of every two marriages ends in divorce and that one day they might be involved in one of these battles. They may be the one of the one in every five children in the United States who goes to sleep hungry every day and who may not have any food on the weekends.

Regardless of the issue, students must learn how to communicate their ideas and feelings to others. By having students role-play situations, they can avoid personal involvement even if the problem is one that they themselves are facing. In each session, an issue will be presented; the issue will be discussed; if necessary, role-players will perform a scripted scenario; students will be given the opportunity to comment; solutions will be proposed; and conclusions will be drawn. The leader of the session should control the conversation and should record the problems, the relevant ideas associated with the problems, and solutions that are satisfactory to all. All sessions should conclude with the students writing a paragraph or two based on all the information disseminated in the session. These compositions should state the problem(s), cite some of the discussion items, and conclude with a recommendation to solve one or more of the problems.

Teen Problems and How Adults Can Help Solve Them is divided into three sections. Section 1 deals with bullying issues. Section 2 deals with puberty issues. Section 3 deals with general issues faced by teens. The topics should be presented to the student, followed by encouragement to discuss the issues based on real-life experiences, either their own or others'. If this strategy fails, then the leader should choose people to read the script and role-play the situation. (The leader may take the role of one of the characters when keeping the conversation private.) The leader should give the role-players ample time to prepare, allowing them to rehearse their parts in the role-play so that they deliver their lines smoothly and with appropriate emotion. When the presentation is finished, the leader should encourage everyone to respond to the script and express how they would handle the situation.

While the discussion proceeds, the leader should note relevant facts related to the problem(s) at hand, any relevant comments that are made, and any solutions that are proposed, and offer a conclusion highlighting the suggested solutions.

Each lesson is presented in five parts. The first part is a discussion of the topic of the lesson. The second part is identification of the problem. The third part list comments, most of which in *Teen Problems and How Adults Can Help Solve Them* are taken from my own students in the past, but some of which are my own comments. The fourth part entails possible solutions to the problem(s) identified. The fifth and final part is to compose a paragraph (or two or three) to summarize the problem(s), note any commentary, and present the solutions that promise to be of help to the teen.

Using the lesson "My Best Friend Called Me Fat," I will give an example of how a lesson should be run. With the topic being a best friend calling a fellow teen fat, during the discussion, other problems might arise and should be added to the list. In this lesson, these other problems are provided in the form of questions: "Why was my friend so cruel?"; "If I am overweight, how can I lose the extra pounds?"; "If I choose to diet, which one should I go on?"; "Which foods are healthy, and will they help me lose weight?"; and/or "Do I need to keep a chart of the foods I eat, and will that limit my food intake?" The leader may guide the teen to ask such questions and explore any problems relevant to the topic.

During the discussion, list only the important comments, in this case, "We should be more considerate of the feelings of others"; "You should tell your friend that she hurt your feelings"; "You are the only one who can take weight off"; "Fast foods have fat and calories but little nutrition"; "Diets help people lose weight"; "Talk to your parents about getting healthier foods in the house (and tell them not to bring snacks into the house)"; "See a doctor to find a diet"; and "My parents exercise to keep their weight down."

Next, list the solutions that have been arrived at by way of discussion. For this lesson, the entries include, "If you feel you are fat, you need to lose weight"; "To lose weight, you can go on a diet"; "You should see a doctor to make sure you don't hurt your body dieting"; "You should talk to your friend and ask her to be more considerate of your feelings in the future"; "Don't eat fast foods, and be sure that what you do eat is good for you"; "You should stop eating junky snacks and eat only healthy foods"; and "You should begin to exercise."

The final part of the lesson is for the students to compose a paragraph (or two or three) summarizing all the points of the lesson: the problem(s) identified, some of the comments made, and some of the solutions to the problem(s).

Parent Permission Letter

Dear Parents,

Your child is about to embark on a health education curriculum that is designed to teach him or her to be safe, build his or her self-esteem, and help him or her make decisions that will help him or her become a responsible adult. The curriculum is not designed to usurp your influence as a responsible parent but to allow your child to share his or her opinions with his or her peers. (Peer pressure is often condemned as being negative, but it can be just as effective in a positive way.)

The purpose of these lessons is to expose your child to problems that he or she is likely to face at school, in his or her social life, and even at home. The problems will be explored, discussed at length by your child and his or her peers, and solved by consensus.

We cannot protect your children from facing many of the problems of growing up in today's society, but *together* we can prepare them for this task. Your interest, support, and caring interaction will assist your child in arriving at healthy attitudes and skills.

Sincerely,

[Teacher or other leader]

Please tear off and return this portion to your child's teacher.

I have read the above letter, and I agree to allow my child to participate in the lessons found in the curriculum entitled *Teen Problems and How Adults Can Help Solve Them.*

_____   _____

Parent's signature   Date

SECTION I
BULLYING

A Discussion of Bullying

The leader might decide to make this discussion a separate lesson.

There is little doubt that bullying is a major problem, affecting students of all ages. It may take the form of making threats, spreading rumors, attacking someone verbally and/or physically, and excluding someone from a group. Bullying may happen in person or through the use of electronic technology (cyberbullying), which can take the form of text messages, emails, pictures, videos, or websites. The desired result is to gain power over the victim.

Students can be bullied themselves, may do the bullying, may witness the bullying, or may serve in one of several roles in relation to the aggressor(s). All can be negatively affected by bullying in many ways. The most negative effects include mental illness, seeking escape through substance abuse, and possibly committing suicide.

Bullying is usually aimed at those who are different from the norm. Children who may be at greater risk include gays, those with disabilities, minorities, and those who are socially isolated. These groups must be monitored with extra care because they may not feel that they are in a friendly environment.

There are definite signs of bullying, but not all students will blame others or ask for help. Some may blame themselves for being bullied and seek a negative solution.

Bullying can be prevented by teaching courses such as this one, building a safe environment, and involving the entire community. (Adults don't like to be bullied in the workplace, and students shouldn't tolerate it at school.) Students should be made aware of what bullying is, learn how to communicate with adults when threatened, learn self-respect, and treat others the way they would like to be treated.

The staff at school is the first line of prevention. It is the staff's job to make sure that all students know what bullying is and how to recognize the warning signs, for example, suffering grades or personality changes. The staff must involve the entire community (especially a victim's parents), get the student to come forward, change the attitude of the attacker, involve the attacker's parents, and change attitudes of all who tolerate aggressive behaviors.

Adults must respond immediately and responsibly to aggressive behavior. It must be made known that it will not be tolerated and will be punished. Adults must know how to get help for victims and stop bullying on the spot. They must also support all students who are involved, make sure the bullying doesn't continue, and make sure its effects are minimized.

Bullying is a destructive behavior that can lead to many types of injury. It is important that those who help victims are well familiar with all the resources available to prevent bullying, stop bullying, and change attitudes toward bullying. These resources are available online and through health professionals. There will be several other examples of bullying in *Teen Problems and How Adults Can Help Solve Them*. These lessons should be emphasized and followed by discussions similar to the one above.

"Why Did You Do That?"

Objective

This is the first of several bullying lessons that will be presented in *Teen Problems and How Adults Can Help Solve Them*. In this case, we will be talking about rumors and understanding that a rumor can hurt others and can be used to spread a lie.

Admissionsly (an agency that discusses bullying) has published the following statistics: 29 percent of all students are bullied in the classroom by teachers and other students, and 29 percent of students are bullied in the halls or cafeteria. The types of bullying show that 13 percent of these students were made fun of. Another 13 percent were subjected to rumors started against them (more girls than boys). Students were cyberbullied 37 percent of the time by the year 2019.

Script

ELAINE   Hi, June. What's up?

JUNE   I'm glad you're back in school today.

ELAINE   I was only out for one day. Why are you concerned?

JUNE   Well, I saw what happened in the gym the other day.

ELAINE   What do you mean?

JUNE   While the teacher was searching our hair for lice, I saw that he took a long time checking your scalp and a long time talking to you, and then you were absent the next day. I assumed he found nits in your hair and told you to stay home until you got rid of them.

ELAINE   But that is not true. My mother bought a new shampoo that I used Sunday in my shower. It irritated my scalp, turning it red and sore. The teacher saw this and recommended that I use a cream to reduce the pain and redness. That's what I did all day yesterday.

JUNE   Oops!

ELAINE   What does "oops" mean? You didn't tell anybody I had lice, did you?

JUNE   Well, not exactly.

ELAINE   What did you do?

JUNE   I mentioned to some students how long the teacher took to check your head, and how long he spoke to you, and—

ELAINE   Why did you do that? Why didn't you call me to ask why I was absent?

JUNE   I didn't think—

ELAINE You sure didn't. Right now, I'm furious with you. What's worse is what my parents will say when they find out that you accused me of having head lice. Let's ask our classmates how you are going to fix this.

Problems

The problem arises because June made assumptions that hurt Elaine's feelings and then said things that hurt her reputation. June also insulted Elaine's parents by leading everyone to believe that Elaine had head lice. June used the internet to spread the rumor, and everyone got the wrong information. This information will remain for all to see for a very long time.

Comments

- "A person should not say anything without checking the facts first."
- "Everyone who spoke to June thought Elaine had head lice. Even if it were true, that is a private matter to be handled quietly."
- "At one time or another, many students get head lice. It doesn't mean they aren't clean or are careless. Sometimes the lice jump from coat to coat in the wardrobe at school."

Solutions

The situation calls for June to say she is sorry to Elaine. The apology should be in writing, to make sure Elaine knows she is sincere. June needs to ask for forgiveness and express her regrets. She also needs to apologize to Elaine's parents in writing. June needs to tell everyone that she made a mistake and that Elaine had a reaction to shampoo and does not have head lice.

Sample Paragraph

June spread a rumor that hurt Elaine's feelings and reputation. June also insulted Elaine's parents by leading others to believe that Elaine had head lice. A person should not say anything without checking the facts first. June needs to apologize in writing to Elaine and her parents. June needs to tell her classmates of her mistake and give them right facts.

"Show-Off"

Objective

Here is another bullying lesson. During this lesson we begin to explore the dynamics of bullying and seek solutions to neutralize its effects.

Every classroom has at least one: the child who excels, gets good grades with little effort, and causes the other students to be jealous. This student is often resented and in some cases hated. The student who is different serves as a threat to those who cannot match his or her performance. The teacher should try to minimize differences between students in order to keep the peace. If the teacher is not successful, then the exceptional child may experience bullying. Students should be willing to discuss feelings about those who are causing them to be jealous. If the desired result is not obtained, then the following script may be used to stimulate responses:

Script

WANDA   Why won't anybody talk to me?

JUNE   What do you mean?

WANDA   I went to lunch and no one would sit at my table. I tried to talk to several of our classmates, but they ignored me. What happened?

JUNE   I heard that our classmates are mad at you.

WANDA   Why? What did I do?

JUNE   I saw your math test score. How did you get a 98 percent on the test?

WANDA   What do you mean? I studied my butt off. I worked hard for that grade. Why would anyone get angry about that?

JUNE   Well, it was ten points higher than anyone else. The real problem is that you get those grades in every subject. When you get high grades, it makes the rest of us look stupid. It even lowers our grades when the teacher figures our averages.

WANDA   You can't expect me to fail my tests so everyone else looks better. I am very proud of what I'm accomplishing, and so are my parents. I want to be a success and make a lot of money so I can live a better life than my parents.

JUNE   All we know is that we have to suffer because you are a genius. That is why everyone is angry with you. Everyone thinks you are a show-off.

WANDA   I am not showing off. I am doing my work like everyone else. If the work I do gets me better grades, it is not my fault. I am not cheating or doing anything wrong. I want to tell the teacher that I have been bullied. I also want to know who started the silent treatment. You have no idea how it feels to think that everyone hates you. I want to go home and never come back to this school.

JUNE   All the students were upset. We have had smart kids in all our grades. It is important that those who do good work should not be punished because of those who, like you, do exceptionally well.

WANDA   I agree. It is up to the teacher to give credit to everyone who works hard, even if they don't get 100 percent on their tests. But it is not fair to call me a show-off and refuse to talk to me. I want it stopped.

JUNE   I hear you, and I feel that our classmates are being unfair. Let's see what they have to say and how the teacher will deal with the problem.

Problems

Students who get high grades are sometimes seen as "show-offs." The teacher needs to do other things to help those who work hard in class. Students are ignoring other students because the latter get higher grades. The silent treatment is being used as a form of bullying.

Comments

- "It is not fair to be angry with someone because they get good grades."
- "The silent treatment is a form of bullying, and it hurts people."
- "Maybe the teacher can give Wanda her A but leave the grade out of the class average."

Solutions

- The class should all apologize to Wanda. They hurt her feelings when it wasn't her fault.
- The students should ask the teacher about a fair solution.
- The students should all try harder to get better grades. They should form study groups.

Sample Paragraph

Should students ignore classmates because they are doing better in their studies? The silent treatment is a form of bullying, and we should not be doing it. Students who work hard and get better grades should not be punished. The teacher should be asked to come up with a fair solution to the problem. Students should try harder to get better grades. Maybe the students should form study groups.

"What Kind of Party Is This?"

Objective

Teen students are often invited to social gatherings and parties, which allow students to relax and have fun, help promote communication, and serve to build friendships. With thirty students in a class and other friends and relatives, students may be attending birthday parties and other parties very frequently. The problem with parties is that they involve the opportunity for substance abuse. The host might have access to the family liquor cabinet, or a friend might produce a joint or other drugs. Most hosts don't want their parents around, so parental controls might be lax or nonexistent.

Chances are, sooner or later, a student will be put in a situation where he or she will be offered a drug. How the student reacts is critical to his or her future with drugs and to his or her self-esteem.

Students may be reluctant to discuss this matter in class, so it might be necessary for the teacher to fabricate a story about a former student who was offered drugs at a party and didn't know how to react. The teacher should ask how his or her students would react and launch into a discussion about how the students feel about drugs.

If all else fails, the teacher may assign the following script:

Script

JOYCE   Hey, Janice, how was your cousin's birthday party?

JANICE   It was weird.

JOYCE   Why, what happened?

JANICE   Everything was going great. We danced, talked, flirted, and sang "Happy Birthday." We were all having a good time until one of my cousin's friends suggested that we go outside in the backyard. Once we were out, there two of my cousin's friends pulled out joints and lit up. They started passing them around, and everyone was taking a hit.

JOYCE   What happened when one got to you?

JANICE   I refused to smoke it and passed it to the person next to me. Everyone started laughing and called me a chicken. After that, things got ugly. Some of the guys took a lot of hits. One of them tried to kiss the girl next to me. Another one went to a tree and vomited.

JOYCE   Nasty. What did you do then?

JANICE   I told my cousin I was leaving, and I bailed.

JOYCE   Did you tell your parents?

JANICE   I didn't have to. The minute I walked in my house, my parents smelled the pot on my clothes.

JOYCE   What did they do to you?

JANICE   They kept talking to me to see that I was not stoned. Then they made me swear to them that I did not smoke. My mother called my aunt to ask if she knew her son was smoking weed. My aunt was not aware of what went on, but she promised to talk to my cousin about making fun of those who didn't want to smoke. She said that since recreational marijuana is legal in this state, all the kids are raiding their parents' stashes and getting high.

JOYCE   Are you kidding? It sounds like your cousin's family smokes together.

JANICE   I wouldn't be surprised, but I don't get it. My parents told me they used to smoke weed but couldn't function for a long time afterward.

JOYCE   My parents told me they never smoked pot, and they think it leads to drug addiction.

JANICE   I don't know if that's true, but I don't see any reason to use drugs unless I'm sick.

JOYCE   I wonder how our classmates feel about the use of drugs?

Problems

Many students are invited to parties. If parental controls are lax or missing, substance use may be occur.

Students who abuse alcohol or drugs may hurt others.

Students may be criticized if they choose not to take drugs or drink alcohol.

Parents have responsibilities when they allow their children to hold a party.

If there is underage substance use at a party, the authorities could be notified.

Comments

- "What should we do if drugs are present at a party?"
- "My friend told me she left a party as soon as the kids started asking if anyone had a joint."
- "Maybe we should ask the host if parents will be around."
- "I always go with a friend who agrees to leave with me if something goes wrong."
- "The teacher should give us a lesson on the dangers of substance abuse, the importance of self-esteem, and how to reject any offer of anything we don't wish to participate in."

Solutions

- Students are invited to many birthday parties and celebrations. They need to be aware that these events can cause problems and promote substance abuse.
- Students can take several steps to avoid getting into an uncomfortable situation. They can ask teachers and parents to discuss self-esteem, what can happen at parties, and what to do if a bad situation arises.
- Students can go to these events with a friend who will support a decision to leave.
- Students can check parental controls at a party or event. If parents won't be present, there is cause for concern.
- Students must understand that it is acceptable to refuse drugs and alcohol. They must understand the dangers and pitfalls of addiction so they can feel confident in avoiding danger.

Sample Paragraph

Many students are invited to parties. If there are drugs at the party, some students can get hurt. Parents have responsibilities when they allow their children to have a party. Students should ask the host if his or her parents will be around. They should also have a plan of what to do if there are drugs at the party, such as go with a friend who agrees to leave with them if something goes wrong. Students must understand that it is acceptable to refuse drugs and alcohol. They must be taught the pitfalls of addiction so that they can feel confident in avoiding danger.

"Please Don't Send Me to the Bathroom"

Objective

This is a serious bullying lesson. Schools have cliques. Some cliques may actually be gangs, which often draw their strength by terrorizing students. Psychologically, everyone has the need to obtain power. When followers encourage the rise of a leader, they create a gang that can cause great damage to one student or a group of students who are weaker in terms of number or age.

Every day children are victimized in cafeterias, gyms, bathrooms, schoolyards, and buses and on the street. Intimidation can be physical or verbal and is reinforced by other members of the group. Such students are usually threatened with physical harm or retribution against friends or siblings. These threats are terrifying, so children usually follow the directives and don't tell anyone about the intimidation. Bullying usually requires the victim to give the gang money or lunch food, allow them to copy homework, do assignments or errands for them, or help them to intimidate others.

Results of this form of bullying can vary, but they are always devastating to the victim. The young teen who is attacked panics every time he or she sees the bully or any member of the gang. He or she may also be traumatized by the thought of meeting the gang at any location on school grounds. The victimized teem must also deal with the consequences of losing lunch money or food, allowing someone else to copy his or her work, or helping the bullies to go after friends or family members.

There is no doubt that students who are threatened will be unwilling to discuss the pressure that was forced on them. The threat of retaliation from a gang will clearly prevent any discussions of bullying. If this is the case, then the teacher may wish to assign the following script to stimulate the conversation:

Script

PETER   What is wrong with you, Charlie?

CHARLIE   l need to go to the bathroom.

PETER   So, raise your hand and ask for permission.

CHARLIE   Can you come with me, please?

PETER   If you want me to. What is the problem?

CHARLIE   l just don't want to go alone.

PETER   Seriously, why would you want me to watch you going to the bathroom?

CHARLIE   l have a problem, and I can't go alone.

PETER   What is the problem?

CHARLIE   Every time I use the bathroom, Jack's cousin comes in with two of his friends, and they rough me up.

PETER   Really? What did you do to Jack that got his cousin mad at you? How does his cousin know when you use the bathroom? How do they rough you up?

CHARLIE   Jack once asked to copy my homework, and I told him he couldn't. He got mad and told his older cousin. I'm not sure how they know when I use the bathroom. When I am here in the cafeteria or the schoolyard, they can see me leaving. When I leave the classroom, maybe Jack sends his cousin a message on his phone, because they always show up while I'm using the bathroom. When they come in, they push me around, punch me, take my lunch money, and threaten to hurt my little sister who is in kindergarten.

PETER   Wow. That sucks. Did you tell anyone?

CHARLIE   I can't say anything. I'm afraid they will hurt my little sister. I told them they didn't scare me, and they punched and kicked me until I was black and blue.

PETER   What do you do when they take your lunch money?

CHARLIE   I watch our classmates and eat whatever they don't.

PETER   That's why you keep asking me if I am eating my lunch.

CHARLIE   Yes. I'm scared. I wake up during the night and imagine that I'm being punched and kicked and that they are hitting my little sister. If you were me, what would you do?

PETER   I would be terrified, but I could not live with nightmares and fear of going to the bathroom. I would have to tell my parents and let them decide who needs to know what is going on. In the meantime, I will go to the bathroom with you, and if anyone threatens or hits me, I'll start a war.

CHARLIE   Thanks, Pete. I don't like being bullied, but I didn't know what to do. I will tell my parents what is happening, and let them handle the threats from Jack's cousin. I wonder what our classmates would do?

Problems

People who threaten others must be punished.
Charlie is being bullied. He is afraid to say anything because he has been hit and threatened. His money has been stolen, and his little sister may be in danger.
Victims suffer from both physical and mental problems.
The power of bullies comes from others who allow them to get away with establishing their power through intimidation.
Those who threaten others must be punished.
Charlie's friend Peter now knows about the problem. Perhaps he should help?

Comments

- "I once told a classmate he couldn't copy from me during a test, and he slashed the tires on my bike. My parents called his parents and straightened it out. He apologized."
- "My parents told me never to let anyone hit me. They told me to go straight to the teacher if anyone ever threatened me at school."
- "I understand why Charlie didn't tell anyone about the threats. He was afraid they would hurt his younger sister."

Solutions

- People who threaten or hurt others must be punished.
- Telling Peter about his problem isn't enough of a response. Charlie needs to tell his parents, his teacher, and the principal that he and his sister are being threatened.
- The bullies need to be punished and also watched to make sure they are not threatening anyone else.

Sample Paragraph

People who threaten others should be punished. Charlie is being bullied, but he is afraid to say anything because he has been hit and threatened. His money has been stolen and his sister may be in danger. Victims of bullying suffer from physical and mental problems. I understand why Charlie was afraid to tell anyone: because he was worried about his sister. The power of bullies comes from others who allow them to get away with establishing their power through intimidation. Telling Peter about his problem wasn't enough of a response. Charlie needs to tell his parents, his teacher, and the principal that he and his sister were threatened. The bullies need to be punished and watched to make sure they are not threatening anyone else.

"I Didn't Do It"

Discussion

This lesson presets a sensitive topic that needs to be addressed with care as it is a topic of great importance to every young teen.

Child abuse is a major problem throughout the world. In the United States alone, more than three million children are abused annually. Child abuse need not be just physical; often a child is also hurt mentally. In either case, the effects can be devastating to a young teen, often lasting a lifetime. Even more alarming is the fact that abuse can be passed down from generation to generation.

Abuse can come from a variety of sources, for example, parents, siblings, relatives, classmates, teachers, and even health professionals who might have prejudices. In some cases abuse can be perceived by a child even if none has occurred. (I remember a situation when my daughter had been denied something she really wanted. She threatened to call the abuse hotline on me and my wife because we wouldn't give her what she wanted.) Another issue to be dealt with is the guilt that some children feel. If children are abused for doing something wrong, they often blame themselves for the infraction(s). This blame can be internalized and manifest itself as permanent damage.

This topic is extremely sensitive, and the last person one would want to be the leader of this lesson is an abuser. Parents should disqualify themselves from discussing how their children feel. They should survey their child to find a responsible sibling or relative who could be impartial to the issues raised by their student. They must have a good rapport with the young teen and understand the implications and what to do if abuse is suspected. If doubts arise, the leader must know whom to contact to confirm the situation.

If desired conversations cannot be elicited, then the following script should help to stimulate talk about abuse:

Script

HEATHER   Luz, why are you wearing pants and a long-sleeve blouse when it feels like it's a hundred degrees outside? You have to be sweltering in those clothes.

LUZ   My mom didn't do the laundry yesterday, so I wore these because they were clean.

HEATHER   You're going to sweat when we go to gym.

LUZ   I'm going to skip gym today. My muscles are sore, so I asked the teacher if I could study while the rest of the class is in gym.

HEATHER   Is that why you are limping and why you sat down so carefully? What really happened, Luz? You can tell me.

LUZ   I fell down the steps in my house. I have bruises on my arms and legs.

HEATHER   That's what I told the teacher when my dad caught me taking money from his wallet. Luckily, my mom stepped in and prevented him from hurting me seriously. Listen, we've been friends for a long time. You can tell me what really happened.

LUZ   My little brother broke a vase in the living room. I was cleaning it up when my dad came home. He thought I did it and started screaming and swinging.

HEATHER   Why didn't you tell him that you didn't break the vase?

LUZ   If I did, he would have gone after my brother. I didn't want that to happen.

HEATHER   So, you took a beating for something you didn't do?

LUZ   I would do anything to protect my little brother and sister. I understand my father's problem, but they don't. They would think he hates them, but he doesn't.

HEATHER   You need to tell someone who can help you to stop the abuse. Whom have you told about what happened?

LUZ   My mother knows, but if she tells, he'll beat her too. What did you do when your father hit you?

HEATHER   The teacher saw my bruises and called in a social worker. The social worker forced my dad to take some courses at a hospital. He goes back every few months and has been good ever since. Maybe you should talk to our teacher and see what happens.

LUZ   I don't know if I want her to know about this. What if she tells someone and my father finds out?

HEATHER   I had the same thoughts, but the teacher told me that anything I told her must be kept confidential by law. She told me that if I didn't want to tell anyone at school, I could call one of the 1-800 hotlines.

LUZ   How do they work?

HEATHER   The teacher told me that by calling Childhelp or one of the other agencies, they will get help to you and your dad so that the abuse stops. It sounded too complicated to me, so I trusted the teacher. Everything turned out fine.

Problems

Luz's body is covered with bruises.
Luz is being abused by her father.
Luz's father beats her when things go wrong.
Luz takes beatings to protect her siblings when they do something wrong.
Luz is afraid that if she complains to her mother, her father will abuse her mother too.

Comments

- "No one should be abused."
- "Everyone makes mistakes, but no one should not be hurt because of them."
- "Luz needs to get help to stop her abuse. She needs to tell someone about the beatings, and she needs to see a doctor to make sure she is not hurt. She should also talk to the teacher or call a 1-800 number to tell someone what is going on."
- "Luz's father needs to see a doctor who can help him stop hurting his family."

Solutions

- Luz has to talk to the teacher to report her abuse.
- Luz needs to tell her father that if he hits her again, she will call the police.
- Luz needs to tell all her relatives what is going on so they can lend support.

Sample Paragraph

Luz's body is covered with bruises. Luz's father beats her when he thinks she has done something wrong. No one should be abused. Luz needs to get help to stop her abuse. She needs to see a doctor to make sure she is not hurt. Her father needs to see a doctor who can help him stop hurting his family. Luz needs to talk to her teacher to report the abuse, and she needs to tell her father that if he hits her again, she will call the police. She also needs to tell her relatives so they lend support.

"My Sister Is in Trouble"

Discussion

Young teens are often influenced by older siblings. Many times, an older sibling serves as a role model for a younger brother or sister. The usual effect (when guided by parents) is positive on younger children. Older children use their knowledge and experience to teach and influence their younger siblings. Working parents often rely on older siblings to supervise and influence their younger siblings.

Inevitably, an older child will get into trouble, and this problem can affect younger teens. Allison's older sister Diane is a case in point. Diane is an eighteen-year-old high school senior whose hormones are raging. She has always guided Allison, helping her with her homework, sharing her stories about school and dating, and encouraging her to follow in her footsteps.

On a recent date, Diane attended a party at the house of a boy whose parents were away for the weekend. There was alcohol, and the party broke up until only Diane and the boy were left in his house. The boy tried to convince Diane to have sex with him, but she resisted. He kept insisting, and Diane ran out of the house. She called her father to pick her up, and when she got home, the war began.

Diane had alcohol on her breath, and she was shaking in fear of almost being raped. Her father was furious that she had been drinking and that she didn't have the sense to leave the house when the last partygoer left. Diane realized that her father was right on both issues and simply cried while he ranted. The house was in chaos, and no one could escape the yelling. When he told Diane to go to her room, he called Allison into the room and started yelling at her. He told Allison that she needed to learn from her sister's mistakes, adding that he never wanted Allison to be in a similar situation. Allison was scared, and she too cried through the whole lecture. She felt that she was being accused of doing something wrong. She didn't say a word, just wept the entire time her father was yelling at her.

Health professionals must illustrate the problems that young teens face today more than ever. Students must and can avoid situations like the one Diane was in. Diane's using her cell phone got her out of that situation. The cell phone is a tool that can be a key to help anyone who finds themselves in a compromising situation.

The purpose of this story is to prevent teens from getting into bad circumstances. A health professional must be armed with the many situations that can occur in the life of a young teen such as dealing with death, bad health, divorce, peer pressure, and bullying, among other things. The hope is that students will respond and discuss problems openly and honestly. If the professional does not get the cooperation desired, then the following script may be used:

Script

KIM   Why are your eyes so red, Allison?

ALLISON   I've been crying all night.

KIM   Why, what happened?

ALLISON   My older sister Diane went to a party, got drunk, and was almost raped. Luckily she ran out of the house and called my father to pick her up. When he smelled liquor on her breath and heard that she allowed herself to be alone with a boy in his house, he spent hours yelling at her and then warned me that I had better not get into a similar situation.

KIM   Why did he yell at you?

ALLISON   My older sister told my dad that my body has changed and that I am now a woman. He wanted to make sure that I didn't make the same mistakes Diane made.

KIM   Your father is a smart man. Remember our talk last week when you told me how hot John was? You told me you wouldn't mind being locked in a room with him for a few hours.

ALLISON   John is hot. But at my age, I would never allow anyone to touch me.

KIM   I'm sure you know that, but knowing you are a woman now might give your dad some doubts.

ALLISON   I guess you're right. How do I let my dad know that I won't make the same mistake?

KIM   Tell him you've been talking to your sister and friends. Tell him you are aware of what Diane did wrong and that you would never go to a party without a friend. In fact, tell him that you'll talk to someone whenever you have any problem that bothers you. Then, make sure you follow your own advice. Chances are, I'll have similar problems and we will be able to hang out together.

ALLISON   I wonder if our guidance counselor or classmates have heard of similar problems. Let's ask.

Problems

Diane got herself into trouble, but luckily she got out of it without getting hurt. Diane must take steps to never let such a thing happen again.

Diane's father yelled at her, and then he yelled at Allison even though Allison had done nothing wrong.

Allison was blamed for her sister's mistake when she was innocent. She must, however, use this as a lesson so she never finds herself in Diane's position.

Diane and Allison should get counseling to deal with their raging hormones.

Comments

- "I know how Allison feels. Every time my siblings break something in the house, I get blamed for not watching them more carefully."
- "My older sister cannot go anywhere without taking a friend or adult with her."
- "Diane must think of ways to avoid dangerous situations."
- "Diane should not have been drinking."

Solutions

- Their father should not have blamed Allison for Diane's mistake. He should have discussed the mistake with Allison so that she would not do the same thing.
- Diane should sit with a counselor to help her deal with her mistake and prevent such a thing from happening again.
- Allison should get counseling to deal with her raging hormones and prevent the same problem from happening to her.
- Girls should establish friendships to prevent them from being alone with a boy. They should also have someone to talk out their problems with.

Sample Paragraphs

Diane got herself into trouble. But luckily she got out of it without getting hurt. Diane must take steps to never let such a thing happen again. Allison was blamed for her sister's mistake, when she was innocent. She must, however, use this as a lesson so that she never finds herself in Diane's position.

I know how Allison feels. Every time mv siblings break something in the house, I get blamed for not watching them more carefully. My older sister cannot go anywhere without taking a friend or adult with her.

Diane should sit with a counselor to help her deal with her mistake and prevent such a thing from happening again. Allison should get counseling to deal with her raging hormones and prevent the same problem from happening to her.

"I Am Going to Sit Next to You"

Discussion

The next moral issue to be discussed involves testing. Education has shifted its focus from learning to passing tests. This creates problems for both teachers and students.

The district in which I was an administrator found out what company was providing our schools with year-end math and reading tests. The district then ordered review books, prepared by the same company, featuring past tests and review materials. When they arrived, teachers were instructed to devote considerable time to these materials so students would be prepared to take the important tests. The message to students was obvious: *Testing is important to your future!* This encourages students to do anything possible to pass these tests. (One has to wonder what effect this attitude has had on the principals of education.)

A second story further illustrates this point. A good test-taker in a prominent high school graduated with a B average. She was proud of her accomplishments and decided to begin her college education at a junior college. When she applied, she was given an aptitude test to determine her proficiency. The results were devastating. She was told that her skills were so weak that she would need remedial courses in both reading and math before she would be allowed to register for college-level courses. The student was bewildered since she had done so well on her tests.

What are students to do if they are not good test-takers? Is cheating a solution? The recent indictments for those who were admitted to prominent colleges because people cheated for them on their SATs further illustrate how bad things have become.

A discussion about these stories should bring up the moral issue of doing anything necessary to get ahead. The health professional or other leader should elicit comments about the stories just discussed. It is important to understand how students feel about the importance of testing versus concept education. The health professional or other leader also needs to know how students feel about current curricula. Do they feel that what they are learning is relevant?

Students should have no problems reacting to these questions, but if the discussion stalls, the following script should be acted out:

Script

ALLISON   Hey, Jason, are you ready for tomorrow's test? I have been studying for weeks to get ready.

JASON   I can't believe how much importance the teacher has placed on this test. I am more interested in the topics we didn't cover because we were taking practice tests. I get nervous before a test, and the teacher has put me in a state of panic. I am scared to think that this test will affect my future.

ALLISON I agree that we are missing content in favor of spending lots of time taking practice tests, but this is the standard that determines class placement and what we will learn in the future.

JASON I hear you, but I blank on tests, and I don't want to be punished for blowing a two-hour test when I feel I've learned the material being tested.

ALLISON I hear you, but I can't take the test for you.

JASON Maybe you can. If we sit next to each other and you keep your answer sheet on the right side of your desk, I'll be able to see your answers, and it will help me to do well on the test.

ALLISON You're kidding, right? You want to cheat on the test? If we get caught, we'll both fail.

JASON We won't get caught. The teacher does paperwork while we take the test. If I see her looking up, I'll move my paper to the other side of my desk. I know the stuff; I just can't do well on a test.

ALLISON I wonder what our classmates have to say.

Problems

Many schools base promotion and graduation on student testing.

Some school districts require teachers to teach to the test. This practice takes time away from teaching content.

Too much emphasis is placed on student test results.

Good test results do not mean that all the material has been grasped.

The importance of testing may lead students to decide to cheat.

Comments

- "Spending weeks going over review tests does not teach us anything."
- "Knowing my grades depend on test results makes me very nervous."
- "I panic when taking a test, but it doesn't mean I don't know the material."
- "With pressure to do well on the test, I can see why some kids would cheat."

Solutions

- Limit the number of practice tests.
- Teach the material in class and let students take the tests for homework.
- Work review materials into the regular curriculum.
- Proctor tests to avoid cheating.
- Make tests less important in determining a student's grade.
- Get help for students who claim they can't take tests.

Sample Paragraphs

Too much emphasis is placed on student test results. Many schools base promotion and graduation on student testing. Some schools require teachers to teach to the test. This practice takes time away from teaching content. With this pressure to do well on tests, one can see why some students would cheat.

I panic when taking a test. It doesn't mean I don't know the material. Spending weeks going over review tests does not teach us anything. Schools should make tests less important in determining a student's grade. Teach test-taking skills. Teach the material in class, and let students take the practice tests for homework.

"My Family Saved My Life"

Objective

I have covered many aspects of bullying in *Teen Problems and How Adults Can Help Solve Them*, but the most important line of defense to save our young teens is their parents. Although our teens think they can solve their own problems, parent intervention is necessary. We have discussed how cruel peers can be to those who are considered different from the group. Unfortunately, without help, and with additional pressure caused by tragedies, teen suicide numbers are increasing alarmingly fast. Adults have lived through many critical troubles, but their young teens have not had the experiences to help them overcome the pressures of life.

According to NewsTracker Daily, suicide is the second leading cause of death among teens. An average of thirteen teens commit suicide every day. (These numbers do not reflect the increase caused by the COVID-19 lockdowns and the additional pressures this put on teens.)

One major key to helping teens who are being bullied is found at home. Parents are a necessary factor in reducing the effects of bullying. Parents need to establish a relationship where their teens feel comfortable talking to them. Parents must avoid emotional responses and must ask questions to gain information that can help their teen. They should reward their teen for talking to them, and encourage their teen to share future issues while strengthening the relationship. Parents must make a commitment to help their teens and follow through on their child's opinion. Parents must be sensitive to their teen's fear of retaliation and avoid placing their child at risk. They must arrange for a confrontation in the presence of administrators and/or guidance counselors. Parents must work within the school's framework for bullying and should volunteer to help solve the problem. Parents must make sure that their efforts will result in their child's safety. If their child is drowning in a situation, then they must consider obtaining outside counseling to help their teen. Parents must encourage their teen to find and stick with a friend at school, as this discourages groups from picking on an individual and allows moral support for teens who are bullied. In order to help teens deal with being picked on, parents must emphasize the child's strengths, skills, and positive attributes and encourage their teens to build on those strengths to raise self-confidence. Through all the abuse, parents must keep the lines of communication open. Parents want to form strategies to deal with difficult peer situations. They must listen and communicate with their child every day. Outside counselors (if employed) can give the parents advice and strategies to aid in communicating with their children. Parents must create new relationships so that teens may establish social friendships that can replace those with students who bully. The more friends a teen has, the less likely the chances that he or she will be bullied. Finally, parents must follow up with their child's school to be sure that steps have been taken to resolve the problem of bullying. In extreme cases, parents may have to resort to changing their teen's school. This is the final option that parents can consider in an effort to save their teen.

In the following script, we see an illustration of bullying and how parents come to the rescue:

Script

MAURA   Hi, Marina! How are you?

MARINA   Things aren't great right now.

MAURA   What's wrong?

MARINA   There is a group of classmates who have labeled me and are telling me that I should get lost.

MAURA   Why? What did you do?

MARINA   Nothing. They call me "Melania Trump" and tell me to go to private school.

MAURA   Wow. That's nasty. But to be honest with you, you are one of the most beautiful girls in the school, and your accent does stand out.

MARINA   Lots of people have accents. Why won't anyone be my friend? I've been called a slut and told to go back to my country.

MAURA   Did you tell your parents about being picked on?

MARINA   I told them, and they were all over it. They questioned me for hours. They even took notes. They questioned me about my feelings every time we were together. They contacted the principal to ask about the school's bullying policy. They got the principal to look into the situation and contact those who were taunting me. They wanted to meet with the instigators but were told that it was not possible and that the school would handle the situation. My parents promised they would solve the problem but insisted that I be kept safe while in school. After daily conversations, we agreed that outside counseling would not be necessary. They encouraged me to pick a friend and stay with her while in school so that I would not be alone to be picked on. They encouraged me to pursue my skills and hobbies so that I would have more self-confidence. They made sure I reported the day's events to them every night. They encouraged me to get out with friends to establish more socialization. They also assured me that they would not let the school off the hook until the bullying stopped. When my older brother heard about my problem, he offered to beat the you-know-what out of the boys bothering me.

MAURA   They are amazing. If that doesn't end it, nothing will. By the way, you can consider me your friend, and I will stay with you whenever you need me. Let your parents know that I will be here for you.

MARINA   Thanks. That means a lot to me, and I'm sure we'll have a lot of fun together.

MAURA   I wonder if our friends' parents handle bullying like yours do. I think we should ask them.

Problems

Bullying is a fact of life for young teens. This is especially the case if a teen is different from his or her classmates.

Most parents leave their teens to solve their own problems because things weren't as bad when they were growing up.

Extreme bullying has greatly increased the suicide rate among young teens. (Some teens cannot handle the pressure.)

Comments

- "Marina's parents are doing an amazing job of helping her."
- "I was being bullied, but the school's bullying policy did not help me. I know that bullying is a need for a person or group who wants to gain power, but why can't it be stopped in school?"
- "We are all different in some way. Marina is now one of us and should not be singled out because of her looks or origin."

Solutions

- Parents must be involved in helping bullied children.
- All bullying must be reported to teachers, guidance counselors, parents, and principals as soon as it happens.
- Schools should publish bullying handbooks, defining what bullying is and offering suggestions to parents on how what steps they can take to help their children.
- Principals should hold workshops to educate parents about how to help their children.

Sample Paragraph

When children are bullied, they are often driven to blame themselves and ultimately look to suicide to escape from their misery. Parents must become aware of depression caused by bullying and must help their child to deal with the dangers that could cause them to injure themselves. If necessary, parents must find outside help to prevent their child from getting hurt.

Problems

Comments

Solutions

Sample Paragraph

SECTION II
PUBERTY

"I'm Growing Uglier by the Minute"

Discussion

Teens have many issues as they mature into adulthood. Girls turn to women by growing breasts and menstruating. Boys turn into men by having their voices change, having erections, gaining muscles, and possibly having nocturnal emissions. Both sexes are subject to changes in their skin, and acne is a common problem. As sweat glands become more active, body odor may become prevalent. These changes can cause a variety of reactions ranging from joy to horror. Young teens must come to deal with looking gawky, gangly, hairy, acne-ridden, and different from what they looked like a few months ago. Some young teens come to terms with their changes well, whereas others have emotional problems. Ample breasts may make a girl happy, while another girl's first period can be devastating. Boys turning to men are usually proud of their masculinity. An erection at the wrong time, however, can cause unbearable embarrassment.

Some deal with crises in a logical way. After all, young teens are all sharing similar problems. Others may struggle to come to terms with what is happening. As just mentioned, both sexes are subject to changes in their skin, and acne is a common problem. Another common problem involves changes in weight. Puberty causes weight changes that greatly effect body image. These changes may also cause eating disorders, including anorexia, bulimia, and binge eating. Ninety-five percent of all eating disorders begin at the age of twelve. Any of these disorders can affect a teen's health, mood, relationships, and everyday functioning, although girls are more affected than boys. Boys become more obsessed with being bigger and stronger. Many have an ongoing and pervasive feeling that their bodies are not normal and end up with negative effects that last for a lifetime.

In the following script, two young teens discuss problems they are encountering as they go through puberty:

Script

HALINA   Joey, how are you feeling?

JOEY   I don't know. I've started eating like an animal, and I'm putting on weight. My stomach is giving me fits.

HALINA   Your stomach is giving you fits? I was up all night with cramps. I'm about to get my second period, and I am not happy about it. My mother tells me that I am growing up normally, but I am not looking forward to these monthly catastrophes.

JOEY   Really? Well, two nights ago I woke up to wet sheets. My mother welcomed me to manhood, but I felt like a slob. The thought of it happening with no warning terrifies me. In fact, the only good thing about me becoming a man is that we can talk to each other about these private things.

HALINA Joey, we've been friends since kindergarten. We have grown up together. We've shared everything in our lives until now. Remember when we showed each other our private parts? That's a secret we will take to our graves. Why should things change?

JOEY Well, in case you didn't notice, we're different now. In fact, I've noticed that your breasts are getting bigger. I think that's sexy.

HALINA Really? Maybe you'd like to feel them while they're swelling. You're my friend, not my boyfriend, so keep it in your pants. Besides, I've noticed something about you lately. It's called body odor, and it needs your attention.

JOEY My mother made me aware of it. I just bought a deodorant, and my baths have turned into showers twice a day. Besides my eating problems, I have been sweating like an open faucet.

HALINA Sweat goes away after a shower. My acne embarrasses me all the time. Isn't it amazing how so many in the class are breaking out?

JOEY It's because no one has changed their diet. Our food will become a major issue.

HALINA I've already noticed that I am not as hungry as I used to be, and Joan claims she has stopped eating almost entirely.

JOEY Well, that's better than Christian is doing. Have you noticed how nasty he has become? He challenges everything you say, and he's just looking to start a fight over anything. And Sally is just the opposite. She is moody and doesn't appear to care about anything.

HALINA Don't forget Jose. He is about a foot taller than the rest of us and looks like he weighs about ten pounds.

JOEY Our class has changed from a great group of kids to a circus of misfits.

HALINA You're right, but the sad part about it all is that the craziness is normal.

JOEY I wonder if our classmates feel the same way we do? We should ask them how they are dealing with puberty.

Problems

Students who go through puberty experience major changes to their bodies, including menstruation, breast growth, eating disorders, nocturnal emissions, acne, sweat production, and changes in mental attitude. As their bodies change, teens can become awkward, hairy, oily, and clumsy.

Comments

- "Some young teens can deal with the changes because they have been prepared by parents or have seen the changes in siblings. Others may suffer mental problems that could last for a lifetime."
- "Many students experience large gains in weight and height."
- "Girls become women, and boys become men, and they must learn to behave like adults."

Solutions

- All young teens should get health education counseling from their teachers and school psychologists with regard to their bodily changes.
- Teens should be pointed to specific websites where they can get information about the changes to their bodies.
- Parents should be aware of their children who are going through puberty and should reassure them that their changes are normal.

Sample Paragraph

Students who go through puberty experience major changes to their bodies, including menstruation, breast growth, eating disorders, nocturnal emissions, acne, sweat production, and changes in mental attitude. As their bodies change, teens can become awkward, hairy, oily, and clumsy. Some young teens can deal with the changes because they have been prepared by parents or have seen them in siblings. Others may suffer mental problems that could last for a lifetime. All teens should get health education counseling from the teachers and school psychologists with regard to their bodily changes. Young teens should be pointed to specific websites where they can get information about these changes. Parents should be aware of their children who are going through puberty and should reassure them that their changes are normal.

"My Best Friend Called Me Fat"

Objective

As students become aware of their bodies, they begin to understand the differences between friends, and they wish to be considered one of their peers. These differences stand out and make students feel self-conscious. Extra weight, braces, acne, and other defining differences can make teens self-conscious about their bodies and can cause many types of anxiety. The teacher should introduce these problems and encourage students to discuss how they feel about being different. It is hoped that students will enter into discussions about these problems and offer understanding about how to deal with the differences that their peers are living with in their day-to-day lives. If the teacher feels that students are not being open and honest, or that they are not willing to contribute to the conversation, the teacher may use the following script to jump-start the dialogue.

To preserve anonymity, fictitious names should be used to ensure that students do not confront each other personally. For this lesson, the teacher should choose students who do not have a weight problem.

Script

JOAN Hi, Tomeka! How are you?

TOMEKA I feel awful, and I am mad.

JOAN Why? What happened?

TOMEKA I noticed that Maria did not do as well as I did on our last math test. I suggested that we could study together before the next test.

JOAN What did she say?

TOMEKA She said, "Don't do me any favors, fatty."

JOAN What a cruel thing to say.

TOMEKA Do you think I'm fat?

JOAN It doesn't matter what I think. It's how you feel that counts.

TOMEKA I know I weigh too much, but I can't seem to lose any weight. Both my parents work late, and they bring home fast food almost every night.

JOAN That could be the problem, but there are a lot of reasons why people weigh too much. Maybe the class can help us solve your problem by discussing how they feel about extra pounds.

TOMEKA, *turning toward the class.* Can you help me with my problem?

Problems

The topic is "My best friend called me fat." During the class discussion, other problems might arise to be added to the list, such as the following:

- Friends can be cruel about extra weight.
- If a student is overweight, he or she needs to find out how to lose the extra pounds.
- If a student chooses to diet, he or she needs to know which one to go on.
- Students need to know which foods are healthy and if they will help him or her lose weight.
- Students need to know whether or not to keep a chart of the foods they eat and if doing so will limit their food intake.

These and similar issues will come up in discussion and should be listed. The teacher or other leader may guide students to these issues and any other problems that may be thought relevant.

Comments

- "We should be more considerate of the feelings of others."
- "You should tell a friend that he or she hurt your feelings by calling you fat."
- "You are the only one who can take weight off."
- "Fast foods have fat and calories but little nutrition."
- "Diets help people lose weight."
- "Talk to your parents about getting healthier foods in the house. (Tell them not to bring snacks into the house.) See a doctor to find a diet."
- "My parents exercise to keep their weight down."

Solutions

- If a student legitimately observes that he or she is are fat, then he or she should lose weight. To lose weight, the student can go on a diet.
- The student should see a doctor to make sure he or she doesn't hurt his or her body by dieting.
- A student whose friend calls him or her fat should talk to that friend to make sure he or she is more considerate of the student's feelings in the future.
- Students should not eat fast foods and should be sure that what they do eat is good for them. They should stop eating snacks and eat only healthy foods.
- Students should begin to exercise. They should ask themselves, "Once I start losing weight, how do I keep losing it?"

Sample Paragraph

My best friend called me fat. Why was my friend so cruel? I should tell her she hurt my feelings. If I am overweight, how can I lose the extra pounds? If I choose to diet, which one should I use? Should I see a doctor to find a diet? I shouldn't eat unhealthy snacks or fast food. Maybe I should exercise like my parents do. Once I start losing weight, how should I continue, and when should I stop?

STEPHEN ABRAMOWITZ

"What Do You Mean, I Smell?"

Objective

Teens are at a time in their lives when they have gone through, or are about to go through, puberty. This stage requires a change in health habits. The increased production of hormones and additional perspiration requires more frequent bathing and other health practices. Children may not be aware of the changes occurring to their bodies, with one result being offensive odors.

Script

CAROL   Wasn't gym fun? I love playing soccer.

ELAINE   I agree. It was great, and I'm glad our team won. The only problem was the heat. I am soaking wet.

CAROL   I'm wet too. I can't wait to get home to take a shower.

ELAINE   I take a shower every morning. That way I start every day fresh.

CAROL   Now that our bodies are changing, I shower whenever I need one. Usually I take two quick showers a day during the warm weather, but sometimes I need three.

ELAINE   Are you kidding? I've been taking a shower every morning since I can remember.

CAROL   I have been too, but now that my body is changing, my habits have to change. Haven't you noticed that you sweat more now? I also noticed stronger odors from my feet and other areas of my body. Raise your arms and smell your armpits.

ELAINE   Wow, do I stink. Do you think other people smell me?

CAROL   I sure do, and I can't believe you would wait until tomorrow morning to wash the smell away. The odor will get on your sheets and everything you rub against.

ELAINE   My mother told me that I will soon become a woman and that my whole body will change.

CAROL   Those changes may be starting now. And you need to keep yourself clean or you'll have no friends.

ELAINE   I hear you. Last week I noticed Alvin didn't smell that good after gym. I guess we're all going through our changes.

CAROL   You have that right.

ELAINE   I'll be showering as soon as I get home.

CAROL You might want to think about some help from deodorants, shampoos, and body washes. They help keep the odors covered up for a long time.

ELAINE My mom has lots of those. I'll see which ones work for me. Thanks for making me aware of my problem. I did start to notice friends shying away.

Problems

Gym and outdoor sports can be fun. As one gets older, however, the results can include excessive perspiration, which leaves a person with offensive body odor. This is the case for preteens and teenagers.

Students should become aware of their body changes and the increase in body odor.

Once students are aware of body changes, they should do things to eliminate odors.

Students should seek help from parents or other trusted adults to solve their body odor problems.

Comments

- "My siblings complain that I smell. I tell them to get lost."
- "My parents talked to me about going through puberty and warned me about my body changes and offensive odors."
- "I spoke to my older sister who went through puberty, and she told me what to do."
- "I looked up puberty online and saw a lot of information about body changes."
- "I agree that during warm weather I need to shower more often than once a day."
- "I use strong soap when I bathe and deodorant afterward."

Solutions

- The solution to dealing with changes in one's body is to be informed about what changes will take place. Students can get this information from parents, teachers, siblings, classmates, and the internet.
- Students should take quick showers whenever they need them.
- Students should learn how to use deodorants, shampoos, special soaps, and other aids to keep them fresh and clean. Being and smelling clean makes students feel better and helps them do well.

Sample Paragraph

Most everyone enjoys going to the gym and playing outdoors. These activities cause perspiration, which can leave us with offensive odors. Teenagers face body changes, which can also leave us with offensive odors. What can students do to become aware of body changes and an increase in odors? Once aware of the changes, what can they do to eliminate odors? They can get information from parents, teachers, siblings, classmates, and the internet. Students should take quick showers whenever they need them because being and smelling clean makes them feel better and allows them to do well. Students should learn how to use deodorants, shampoos, special soaps, and other aids to keep themselves fresh and clean.

"My Cousin Is Gay"

Discussion

This lesson is one of the most controversial of *Teen Problems and How Adults Can Help Solve Them*. It deals with a topic that is challenged by both religions and moralists. It is a prominent issue and becomes more widely discussed as more and more people come out of the closet every day. The issue is further complicated by the many different ways we interpret the term *love*. In different ways, we have feelings for our parents, siblings, relatives, friends, and teachers, and other people. The feelings toward all these vary depending on the relationship.

As students go through puberty, they develop sexual feelings. This is a way of life that has been accepted although not totally approved. What has been agreed upon is that love for those of the same sex is not a choice. It is an attraction that can only be fulfilled by physical contact. Students may be forming relationships and developing feelings toward others. At this level, these feelings may not yet be sexual, but for sure the young people are becoming aware of sexual differences and must understand the choices that they may face in the future. These differences are becoming more apparent and will eventually be observed in the world around them.

In the following script, two students discuss a conflict that one of the students has to deal with:

Script

JUNE   I visited my seventeen-year-old cousin's house yesterday, and boy was I surprised.

MICHELLE   Why? What happened?

JUNE   I went to my cousin's room to say hello and found my cousin kissing his boyfriend.

MICHELLE   So, what's wrong with that? I have kissed a boy, and I saw you kissing John on the cheek last week.

JUNE   My cousin's name is David.

MICHELLE   Oh! What did the two of them do when they saw you?

JUNE   They smiled and asked how I was doing.

MICHELLE   What did you do?

JUNE   I told them I was fine and left the room. I went to my aunt and told her that David was kissing a boy in his room.

MICHELLE   What did she say?

JUNE   She told me that they were good friends and that they were different from most teenagers. She told me that David had told her and his father that he had feelings for his friend and cared for him. The two of them are together all the time, and both boys understand the decisions they made, my aunt said. She told me to discuss what I saw with my parents when I get home.

MICHELLE   Did you talk to your parents?

JUNE   l did. My mother told me that my aunt had called her to explain what had happened so that my mom would not be surprised when I got home. Mom told me that she loved my father very much and that they were very attracted to each other. She went on to tell me that sometimes people of the same sex have this attraction and want to be together. She explained that this attraction is a feeling and is not learned. She pointed out that lots of times we see boys and girls holding hands with each other and that they like each other, like you are attracted to Johnny and like she is attracted to my father. It is normal, and today it is accepted by almost everyone.

MICHELLE   Wow, that's heavy. What do you think about what she said?

JUNE   Although my cousin is the first gay person I've known, I have seen many on television, so I guess it does happen. I was shocked, though, to see it in my own family.

MICHELLE   l wonder how others feel about what happened to you. Shall we ask our friends?

Problems

June has discovered that her cousin David is gay.
June has to find a way to deal with this information.
June's mother has to find a way to deal with June's feelings.
June's friends and classmates will have something to say about June's discovery.

Comments

- "Everyone is aware that gays exist. Homosexuality is highlighted on TV and is seen wherever people congregate."
- "Most people treat gays as if they are like everyone else, but I don't understand why some people call gays names. They are people just like the rest of us."
- "Most people know someone who is gay. Homosexual people deserve the same respect that they give us."
- "My favorite cousin is gay. I actually like her more than most of my other relatives."

Solutions

- June should treat her cousin the same way she treats her other relatives.
- June should discuss her issue with her cousin, parents, friends, and classmates to see how they feel about gay people.
- June's mother should be sure that June has all the facts about gay people. Her mother should get books for June so that June can be informed and then form her own opinions.

Sample Paragraph

June has discovered that her cousin David is gay. How will June deal with this information? How will June's mother deal with June's feelings? Everyone is aware that gays exist. Homosexuality is highlighted on TV and is seen wherever people congregate. Most people treat gays as if they are like everyone else, but I don't understand why some people call gays names. They are people just like the rest of us. Most people know someone who is gay. Homosexuals deserve the same respect that they give us. June should discuss her issue with her cousin, parents, friends, and classmates to see how they feel about gay people. June's mother should be sure that June has all the facts about gay people. She should also get books for June so that June can be informed and then form her own opinions.

ADHD or Testosterone?

Discussion

All young teen males go through puberty. It is a stage of life when boys become men by starting to produce testosterone. They mature and begin becoming aware of the opposite sex. Young women produce this hormone as well, with lesser effects. The effect on both is the increased production of bone and muscle mass. When male teens get this surge from their gonads, they often have difficulty paying attention, become hyperactive, and become impulsive. Unfortunately, these symptoms are very similar to ADHD. Attention deficit hyperactivity disorder has now been identified as a problem in the classroom. When these symptoms appear, teachers are often unaware of what is causing them but realize that they are disruptive to teaching. While ADHD often requires medical treatment, the arrival of male puberty does not. The sudden increase in activity can be treated by providing the student with opportunities to work off extra energy.

Script

SALLY   Johnny keeps bothering me. He talks to me and moves things on my desk. He is constantly bothering me.

ADULT   l see that. Others have the same complaint. Johnny, you must leave others alone.

SALLY   l can't get my work done. You have to do something to help me.

ADULT   l have been talking to Johnny's teacher, and she told me that several teachers in Johnny's grade have similar problems with their boys.

JOHNNY   I'm sorry, but it is hard to control my feelings. I can't concentrate and have too much energy.

ADULT   l don't think it is your fault. Your body is changing, and as you go through puberty, the increase in testosterone has made you hyperactive.

Problems

As mentioned in the opening discussion, as young teenage boys go through puberty, they produce large amounts of testosterone. When this takes place, the boys become inattentive, hyperactive, and impulsive. Their behavior changes, and they often bother others and have trouble concentrating on schoolwork. The two issues are how to diagnose the difference between ADHD and how to deal with the increase in hormone production while dealing with similar symptoms from both.

Comments

ADHD is a medical condition that can be treated with medication and therapy. Increased activity due to an increase in testosterone is normal but may be manifested because of similar symptoms. Treatment for increased hormones can be as simple as increasing physical activity. This often reduces hyperactivity and allows young men to concentrate on activities without being disruptive. Working off extra energy often reduces impulsiveness and allows increased attentiveness.

Solutions

In Johnny's case, an increase in physical activity should be the solution. Johnny's parents could decide to rent an exercise bicycle so that Johnny can ride for an hour before going to school. Johnny's parents could agree to pay their son twenty-five cents for every mile he rides. The intended result is to relieve extra tension and energy so that Johnny can better concentrate on his schoolwork. In addition, Johnny could be enrolled in lunchtime and after-school physical activities to further relieve his extra energy. If none of the strategies work, Johnny might be referred to the school's social worker or nurse so that he can be referred for a medical diagnosis of possible ADHD.

Sample Paragraph

When young teenage males go through puberty, they experience an increase in the hormone testosterone. This often causes hyperactivity, impulsiveness, and a lack of ability to pay attention. These symptoms are very similar to those of ADHD and are often confused with similar behaviors. Increased physical activity will help relieve the symptoms. If not, a young teen must be referred to a doctor to see if medical treatment is necessary.

"You Got Your What?"

Discussion

Young teenage girls mature rapidly. They are exposed to womanhood at home, in school, on television, and on the internet. Once their hormones start raging, they turn to friends to solve their curiosity. The ultimate indication of maturity comes when they experience their first menstrual cycle. For some it is devastating. For others it is greeted with the knowledge that it is normal. Some accept the prospect as normal but panic at the sight of blood. Of great importance is the responsibility that comes with womanhood. The need to understand the implications of getting one's first period is most important. A girl must understand how her body has changed. She must also be made aware of what she can expect in the future. Most important, she must understand that she is now producing eggs that can become a child if fertilized by sperm.

Many parents find discussing the topic embarrassing. A student's friends may provide inaccurate information about this important subject. Thus, this most important time in a girl's life must be addressed as a matter of urgency. Accurate information can be obtained on the internet and should be recommended to young teen girls. Talking to one's mother, who has firsthand information about a woman's changes, is also a valuable endeavor.

The following script illustrates a typical conversation between friends and is designed to initiate research to help young teenage girls to cope with their newfound issue:

Script

AMAL   Hi, Lina. How are you?

LINA   I'm OK today.

AMAL   Today? Why, what happened yesterday?

LINA   I was devastated last night.

AMAL   Why, what happened?

LINA   After dinner, I felt cramps and my underpants felt wet, and when I went to the bathroom, I found them full of blood. I called my mother and she told me I was having my first period. I couldn't believe I was bleeding, and I panicked. I had been warned that menstrual cycles start at our age, but looking at that blood shook me up. Have you gotten yours yet?

AMAL   Yes, mine came two months ago. I was in class and felt something wet in my pants. When I got to the bathroom, I found that my underwear was bloody and so were my jeans. Luckily no one could see the blood on my jeans, so I went to the nurse and asked her to call my mother to pick me up. On the way home, Mom stopped at the drugstore and bought me pads to put in my underwear. When I start feeling cramps, I put a pad in my underwear to be ready for when the bleeding starts.

LINA   If it happened at school I would have been crying and screaming for help. How were you so calm?

AMAL   When I turned twelve, my mother showed me articles about menstrual cycles on the internet. I read a number of articles, and although I felt prepared, getting my period in school was quite upsetting.

LINA   My mother tried to calm me be telling me this was not a big deal. She said she welcomes her "friend" every month.

AMAL   Your mother calls her period a "friend"? Anything that gives me cramps, makes me bleed, and makes me smell is not my friend.

LINA   Mom says that if she gets her period, it means she is not pregnant. She told me that I am now making eggs, which could turn into babies if I allow a boy or man to give me his sperm.

AMAL   I got that lecture too. I am not planning on having sex with anyone anytime soon. I do have feelings for boys, but I need to deal with bleeding before I deal with letting any boy have my body.

LINA   I agree. This is traumatic enough without dealing with the thought of having babies.

AMAL   Have you talked to our classmates and friends about their periods? They're all going to get them sooner or later, and maybe they can make you feel more comfortable.

LINA   You helped a lot, but I will talk to our friends and go on the internet to get more information.

Problems

Lina got her first period and was devastated by the blood that she saw in her underwear. Amal got her first period in school and was embarrassed because she had to go home.

Parents are sometimes embarrassed to discuss menstruation, and friends may have inaccurate information, which could be confusing to teens. Girls who get their periods must be taught about the changes that are taking place in their bodies.

Comments

- "After Lina got her period, she noticed that she started to smell. That started a whole new hygiene routine for her."
- "After a few periods, I noticed my breasts were growing huge. My mother had to buy me bigger bras."

- "You can read a whole lot of stuff on the internet. In that way, there are few surprises when your period comes. And some girls have no problem dealing with it."
- "I asked the school nurse questions, and she was very helpful."

Solutions

- Parents should make sure that their daughters are prepared for their first menstrual cycle. Girls should understand what their first period means to their mental attitudes and their bodies.
- Moms are a great resource for young teens seeking to understand their bodies. Having lived through the cycles, a mom can give valuable help.
- The internet can also be of great value in helping teens deal with their periods.
- Discussing issues with friends can provide a teen with the wrong information but can serve as a great emotional aid.
- Teens can obtain help and information from their school nurse or health education coordinator.

Sample Paragraph

Parents should make sure that their daughters are prepared for their first menstrual cycle. Girls who get their periods must be taught about the changes that are taking place in their bodies. Lina got her first period and was devastated by the blood that she saw in her underwear. Amal got her first period in school and was embarrassed because she had to go home. Parents are sometimes embarrassed to discuss menstruation, and friends may have inaccurate information, which could be confusing to teens. There is a great deal of stuff to read on the internet. In that way, there are few surprises when your period comes, which some girls have no problem dealing with. Teens can obtain help and information from their school nurse or health education coordinator. Girls should understand what their first period means to their mental attitudes and their bodies.

"I Loved My Grandma"

Discussion

In life, there are only two things that are for certain: death and taxes. Unfortunately, young teens cannot control either one. A most important part of their lives are the relationships they establish with family. After their parents and siblings, grandparents are usually the most prized people in a teen's life. Grandparents serve as surrogate parents and add gifts, support, love, and nonthreatening experiences to a teen's life. Seldom are grandparents called upon to discipline their grandchildren, which makes them more beloved in the teen's eyes.

For all these reasons. the loss of a cherished grandparent can be particularly devastating. The older a child becomes, the more shocking the loss can be. In many cases, the child loses not only a family member, but a good friend. This loss affects many people, including the teen, his or her parents, the surviving spouse, and other family members. For a young teen, this is often the first loss of life he or she experiences, and it can leave permanent scars.

Although parents should serve as buffers to ease any loss, teens react differently to tragedy with some taking it worse than others. Parents will naturally tell their teens that the lost loved one was a wonderful person who will be sorely missed. The teen, of course, knows this but is in need of solace, sympathy, and emotional support. Given the young age of a teen at the time of the loss, it might be difficult to find friends who can relate to a loss. In this case, the teen must turn to relatives who the teen feels will be able to deal with his or her emotional loss.

In the following script, we see a devastated teen who is talking to a friend who has not experienced the loss of a loved one:

Script

NATASHA   Kim, you look so sad. Is anything wrong?

KIM   My grandmother died recently, and I miss her terribly.

NATASHA   I'm sorry. Was she sick?

KIM   My parents said she had heart trouble. They told me that she had a heart operation three years ago. They never told me what happened, but she seemed OK after the operation. I saw her every weekend, and she always made my favorite meal and told me she loved me. Last week I noticed she was not herself and asked her what was wrong. She told me she had no energy and had to stop every few minutes to rest. When I told my parents, they called her doctor and got an appointment for the next day. When I asked how Grandma was, they said her heart rate had dropped. They told me she was very sick and might need another operation. They said the doctors were going to put a pacemaker near her heart to keep it pumping regularly. After two days, my parents told me the operation didn't work and that Grandma was very sick. I saw her in the hospital, and she told me that she loved me more than anything. Four days later, my parents told me that her heart had stopped and she had gone to heaven. I cried for two days.

NATASHA   That's a bummer. I can't imagine how I would feel if that happened to my grandmother. I see my grandma every weekend, and she always has a present for me.

KIM   I wish I could see my grandmother one more time so I could tell her how much I love her.

NATASHA   My parents told me that when people leave this world, they go to heaven. They said that they can see and hear us from there. When you get home, why don't you go to your room and talk to your grandmother?

KIM   Do you believe I can talk to dead people?

NATASHA   My parents taught me that if I truly believe in something, it can happen. If I lost someone I loved, I would tell that person my feelings every day.

KIM   But she can't answer me.

NATASHA   But you can answer yourself. Sometimes when you say something, you think about what you said and can imagine what the answer would be. If you talk to your grandmother, I'm sure you can imagine what she would have to say.

KIM   I did think about what she would say while she was alive. I guess it would still work now that she is gone. Thanks, Natasha. I feel much better knowing that she will not be far from my thoughts. In fact, when I do things around the house, even my parents say, "Grandma would be so proud of you," showing me that Grandma is still an important figure in our house. I hope she will stay with us forever.

NATASHA   I would think that she will be with you for a very long time. I am sure that others in our class have lost a loved one. Perhaps you should talk to our classmates to see how they feel about the loss of a loved one. You might also talk to the guidance counselor, who I am sure has dealt with many students who have been in the same situation you are in.

KIM   I will. And thanks again.

Problems

Kim lost her grandmother and is very sad about never seeing her again. Sooner or later we all lose a loved one and must deal with the loss in our own way.

If you don't deal with a loss correctly, it can cause scars that can last for a long time.

Young teens are very vulnerable to loss and must seek help the minimize damage to their well-being.

Comments

- "Two of my grandparents died in a car crash. It really hurt to lose them quickly, but parents must help teens to understand that tragedy is part of life."
- "I don't know how I would feel if anything happened to my grandparents. I love them all."
- "My parents tell me that my grandparents are getting older and that I will not have them forever. My parents encourage me to enjoy my elders while I can."
- "If you go to the guidance counselor at school, they can help you deal with your losses."

Solutions

- Kim should receive grief therapy from the school psychologist or an outside therapist.
- Kim's parents should do everything they can to lessen her loss. They should help her to cope by reminding her about the good times she spent with her grandmother.
- Family members should prepare Kim for other losses. She must realize that some losses are natural, whereas others may be sudden.
- Kim should be encouraged to enjoy the time she has with her loved ones.

Sample Paragraph

Kim lost her grandmother and is very sad about never seeing her again. Sooner or later we all lose a loved one and must deal with the loss in our own way. If you don't deal with a loss correctly, it can cause scars that can last for a long time. Young teens are very vulnerable to loss, so we must help to minimize damage to their well-being. It hurts to lose a loved one or a friend quickly, but parents must help teens to understand that tragedy is part of life. Teens should be encouraged by parents to enjoy their elders while they can. A school guidance counselor can help students deal with their losses.

"I Am Different, but I Will Be Fine"

Discussion

Young teens are not immune to adult diseases. In fact, children of all ages can get diseases. When very young, children rely on their parents to keep them healthy. When a young teen is stricken with a life-threatening disease, he or she must deal with it on his or her own.

My friend's daughter went through puberty and suddenly found herself drinking and urinating constantly. She also felt tired. A trip to her doctor and a blood test indicated that she had type 1 diabetes. Her parents panicked, but their daughter understood she was sick and quickly realized what she had to do to get and stay healthy. Her doctor admitted her to a hospital for two days to monitor her condition and determine the amount of insulin needed to keep her feeling well. It took almost a month of trial and error to arrive at a routine that kept the girl healthy and routinized. This involved analyzing every meal and snack that she ate. She then had to determine how much insulin she would need to metabolize the meal she was about to eat. She also had a monitor injected into her arm so she could keep track of her sugar levels at all times. This practice carried over to school in a similar manner. After having breakfast at home, the thirteen-year-old had to find out what the school was offering for lunch and calculate the amount of insulin she would need. Just before lunch, she would have to go to the school nurse and explain her calculations before injecting herself under the supervision of the nurse.

Unfortunately, young teens can contract diseases of all kinds. Some require help from parents and professionals, but many can handle the situation by themselves.

The following script describes a conversation between two students who are aware of problems associated with a disease:

Script

MADISON   Hi, Lilly. How are you? I haven't seen you in school for a few days. Where have you been?

LILLY   l was in the hospital.

MADISON   What happened? Are you all right?

LILLY   l was diagnosed with diabetes, and I am in the middle of getting myself on a routine to keep me feeling well.

MADISON   How did you know you had a problem?

LILLY   l was tired and had to pee every ten minutes. I kept drinking because I was always thirsty. My parents took me to the doctor, and he took some blood. He checked my blood sugar and told me I had diabetes. He sent me to the hospital, where they gave me insulin based on the food that

I ate. For two days they made adjustments and told my parents what to look for when I got home. The nurses gave my parents a list of the carbohydrate content of certain foods and taught them how to calculate how much insulin I would need to keep my sugar levels even. They suggested that my parents order a monitor that could send my sugar levels to my phone whenever I wanted a reading. The nurse also suggested an insulin pen that can deliver the right amount of insulin based on what I eat.

MADISON   It sounds like you have everything under control.

LILLY   Not really. If I calculate my insulin based on what I will eat, I must eat the complete meal or else I will have taken in too much insulin and my blood sugar will be too low.

MADISON   What happens when you come to school?

LILLY   Since I eat breakfast and supper at home, the only meal I need to eat at school is lunch. The nurse will get the menu for me, and I will go to her office before lunch. Based on the menu, I will calculate the amount of insulin I will need to eat the entire meal, and I will dial my insulin pen to the amount I will need to balance my sugar. The nurse will check my figures and watch while I inject myself.

MADISON   What happens if you make a mistake?

LILLY   If my sugar gets too high or too low, my monitor will start to beep, letting me know something is wrong.

MADISON   What happens then?

LILLY   Either the teacher sends me to the nurse with an escort or she calls the nurse to the classroom. When my monitor beeps, it sends a signal to my parents' phones, so they know if I am in trouble, and if I am, they can come to the school.

MADISON   You are not the only one in the class with problems. John has asthma, and he needs to go to the nurse when he has trouble breathing. I wonder if any other students have issues that have to be dealt with. Let's ask the other members of our class.

Problems

Young teens can contract adult diseases.
At times they must deal with their problems the way adults do.
There are additional problems when students must deal with their disease in school.
Classmates must understand the needs of those with diseases and provide them with help and support.

Comments

- "There are many diseases that children can get."
- "My friend had asthma and had an inhaler that he used when he couldn't breathe."
- "My friend had eczema and had bandages on his affected spots."
- "Students can help if they know what is wrong with their classmates."
- "Teachers must be aware of any problems their students might have."
- "It is important that a nurse be present to help students who need help."
- "Children with diseases should do research to be aware of developments with their disease."

Solutions

A young teen must understand the disease that affects him or her, including how to treat it and, if necessary, where to get help. Families, teachers, and nurses must be aware of a student's disease and must know how to help when needed.

Sample Paragraphs

Young teens can contract adult diseases. At times they must deal with their problems the way adults do. Additional problems arise when students must deal with their disease in school. Classmates must understand the needs of those with diseases and provide them with help and support. Students can help if they know what is wrong with their classmates.

Teachers must be aware of any problems their students might have.

It is important that a nurse be present to help students who need help. Children with diseases should do research to be aware of developments with their disease. A young teen must understand the disease that affects him or her, including how to treat it and, if necessary, where to get help. Families, teachers, and nurses must be aware of a student's disease and must know how to help when needed.

"Why Can't I Learn?"

Discussion

Another lesson deals with physical problems that young teens may face. This lesson deals with children who have learning disabilities.

When I began teaching in 1968, all children who could not learn normally were assigned to an age-appropriate CRMD (children with retarded mental development) class. There were few, if any, specific classifications of mental disabilities. If a child was having a really bad day, he or she was sent to the guidance counselor to chill out. If a classroom teacher identified a problem child, the child was referred for testing. If the child did not score well, and if the parents agreed, the child would be placed in an age-appropriate CRMD class.

As time went on, it became obvious that there were different symptoms associated with different learning deficits. In recent years psychologists have given names to those with autism, ADHD, Asperger's syndrome, retardation, etc. In addition to these classifications, we have discovered drugs that can minimize the effects of various mental disabilities. Once a student is diagnosed, parents and teachers must develop a plan to make sure that the student derives the maximum benefit from his or her medication and education.

According to Healthline, 13 percent of males and 4.2 percent of females are diagnosed with ADHD. Males are three times more likely than females to show symptoms. Children with ADHD number 6.4 million. Over the past eight years there has been a 42 percent increase in diagnoses. ADHD has its largest occurrence in six states.

As listed, each disability has its own set of symptoms. These symptoms can give professionals clues about the disability and allow them to begin a plan for both school and home. In the following script, we see a specific set of symptoms that characterize a student who appears to have ADHD, although these symptoms can be indicative of several disabilities. Research can narrow the type of disability, which allows us to set a plan for recovery.

Script

BRANDON   I failed another math test. That is the third test I failed this week. I screwed up the reading and history tests too.

EMILY   Why can't you focus? I can study with you if you want. And why were you talking out during the test?

BRANDON   I don't know. I guess I was frustrated because I didn't understand the questions.

EMILY   But the teacher went over the material yesterday. Why did you keep interrupting her? Did you do the homework, which also covered the material on today's test?

BRANDON   I didn't do the homework because I was watching several game shows. Don't blame me if the homework was stupid. I looked at it, but it made no sense.

EMILY   That's a ridiculous statement. It was a summary of what the teacher said in class yesterday. Why can't you sit still while we are discussing why you are failing?

BRANDON   Stop! I don't want to deal with your stupid accusations, and I don't have to answer to you.

EMILY   You need help. What do your parents think about your pattern of failure?

BRANDON   They keep talking to my teachers, but they agree with me that the work is stupid. Did you see the football game on TV last night? It was great.

EMILY   Why do you keep changing the subject? You do the same thing in class.

BRANDON   If you can't understand me, then I don't need to talk to you. My problem is that I can't concentrate. If people can't understand that, then I don't need to be with them.

EMILY   I realize what your problem is. I remember that Sammy had the same problem when we were in the third grade. He went to special doctors and received medicines and counseling. He is now fine and is doing well in his studies and friendships. I wonder if there are other students in our school who have similar problems. We should ask our classmates if they know anyone else like you.

Problems

Brandon exhibits many of the symptoms associated with attention deficit hyperactivity disorder (ADHD). These symptoms are both mental and physical. His mental symptoms include:

1. making careless mistakes, ignoring details, and being inaccurate in his homework assignments;
2. having trouble paying attention and focusing during class, during conversations, or while reading;
3. appearing not to hear when spoken to directly because his mind is wandering; and
4. not being able to follow directions, quickly losing attention, and being easily sidetracked.

His physical symptoms include:

1. fidgeting, tapping his hands and feet, and squirming in his seat;
2. leaving his seat without permission and not being where he should be;
3. being unable to play quietly and unable to stay still for any extended period;
4. talking excessively and blurting out answers before a question is complete;
5. not waiting for his turn and often moving ahead in line;
6. intruding on conversations, games, or activities; and
7. using other people's possessions without asking or receiving permission.

Comments

In recent years, many mental disabilities have been identified. Most are characterized by specific symptoms. It must be noted, however, that similar symptoms are identifiable in several disabilities. Careful analysis can usually help in planning a treatment that can return a child with a learning disability into a normal functioning child.

One must be aware that symptoms of one disability may be common to several disabilities and that a majority of symptoms could indicate a specific disease.

Solutions

Treatment for mental disabilities is dependent upon the type of deficit. Because symptoms are different and are observed in different degrees in different disabilities, a multifaceted approach is often necessary. Treatment might take the form of training, drug therapy, counseling, or natural therapy, or a combination of some or all.

The first phase of treatment is a comprehensive diagnosis. There are tests for each set of symptoms, and combining these with behavioral analysis and counseling results makes it possible to get an accurate picture of what is necessary to help a student become a success.

Once there is a complete picture of the student and his or her disabilities, a plan of action must be outlined. Assuming the description of the foregoing student matches a diagnosis of ADHD, the family is not only valuable in providing information but also crucial in helping with treatment. With the aid of teachers, counselors, psychologists, and doctors, the following options are most important:

1. brain training to improve concentration and focus;
2. cognitive training to improve attention, memory, auditory analysis, auditory processing, and reading;
3. medical treatment, including the possible use of drug therapy (commonly used drugs include Adderall and Concerta. Many other drugs are now available depending on the symptoms);
4. natural treatment including the use of omega-3 fatty acids;
5. counseling, which could take place in or out of school;
6. psychological treatment in extreme cases.

It is important to note that there is no set recipe for treating disabilities. The foregoing lists are only suggestions and must be treated as such.

Sample Paragraph

Brandon exhibits many of the symptoms associated with attention deficit hyperactivity disorder. These symptoms are both mental and physical. In recent years many mental disabilities have been identified. Most are characterized by specific symptoms. It must be noted, however, that similar symptoms can be identified in several disabilities. Careful analysis can usually help in planning a treatment that can return a child with a learning disability into a normal functioning child. Because symptoms are different and are observed in different degrees in different disabilities, a multifaceted approach is often necessary. Treatment might take the form of training, drug therapy, counseling, or natural therapy, or a combination of some or all.

"But I Like Him"

Discussion

The world is changing. Fifty years ago, interracial marriages were illegal in the United States. Fast-forward to today, and according to the US Census, 17 percent of marriages (11 million) are between people of different ethnic backgrounds. According to Lifehack, 49 percent of Asians marry people of different backgrounds. Today, people judge others for who they are instead of who they represent.

Young teens face additional issues. They have raging hormones, which encourages them to enter relationships based on feelings they establish with the students around them. Most relationships are platonic, but when attractions take hold, the situation becomes more complicated. Young teens do not consider their future or plan their lives based on what is happening currently. This allows students to enter relationships (both platonic and sexual) with little consideration of the consequences. It is not beyond the realm of possibility for young teens to be attracted to one another regardless of their backgrounds or outside influences. Teens from foreign countries who immigrate or visit the United States often awaken curiosities in indigenous teens. Some look different, some talk different, and most have different values. In many cases these differences can prove attractive to students who have never seen them before. Add a pretty face or an exceptional physique to this mix and you have an irresistible draw. Mixing different cultures, however, brings problems that may not be anticipated by teens who are enthralled with each other.

In the following script, a local White girl discusses a new Black student who came from a foreign country. She likes the way he looks, talks, and acts. He is excited to have a local interested in him and looks forward to having his new friend explain things that he does not understand.

Script

DELORES   Hi, Elaine. Did you see John, the new Black boy who joined our class last week?

ELAINE   Did I? I had lunch with him all week. He asked if he could sit next to me at the table. He was so cute, I had trouble eating my lunch.

DELORES   He is good-looking. Where is he from?

ELAINE   Good-looking? He's gorgeous! He is from Darwin, Australia, and has the sweetest accent. I want to keep him talking so I can listen to his speech. He has muscles on his muscles, and his life in Australia was different from the way we live here.

DELORES   How so?

ELAINE   He says it never gets below forty degrees in Australia, so they are outside all year. He also said that 95 percent of the people live on 5 percent of the land, which means that almost everyone in Australia lives in cities. He also said that there is very little crime in his country and that gun ownership is tightly restricted. He says that most of the country is desert and that most cities are near water. He says that almost everyone in his country came from other countries, so they all have different languages and customs. There is very little discrimination, and everyone is treated as an equal. Can you imagine living in such a friendly environment?

DELORES   It sounds too good to be true. Why would he move here when things are so good down there?

ELAINE   He said that his father was assigned to his company's US office and his whole family moved here. I think it's great. I invited him to study with me at my house.

DELORES   Whoa. Calm down. From what you told me, you guys are completely different. Don't get in over your head.

ELAINE   What do you mean?

DELORES   There are many things that you have to consider before you walk this guy down the aisle. Remember that he is racially different from you. From what you have told me, you have completely different value systems. He looks at the world in a healthy way, whereas you live with controversy. This will lead you to make unhealthy assumptions about your life based on how he lives. You will assume his racist attitudes when they are impractical in our country. He will encourage you to ignore racial remarks, when they may be a sign of danger to you. You will ignore our racial boundaries when they may affect him. You may ignore the opinions of others, which could affect your relationship. Worst of all, since he is Black, you may come to assume a superior attitude toward him because of his color. There are many problems that arise from an interracial relationship, and you have to be aware of them.

ELAINE   I hear what you're saying about the issues involved, but eleven million interracial relationships show that all problems can be overcome. Besides, neither of us has discussed walking down the aisle. At this point we are friends who are looking to enjoy each other's company.

DELORES   I have had a crush on two boys so far. Neither led to a serious relationship. Maybe we should discuss the issue with our parents and classmates. What do you think?

Problems

Until fifty years ago, interracial marriages were illegal.

Elaine has fallen for a new Black student, John, who transferred from another country. She thinks he is attractive and is fascinated by his accent and background. She has invited John to her home.

Delores explains differences in their lifestyles in an effort to get Elaine to be objective.

Elaine is not evaluating the situation from a logical perspective.

Comments

- "A lot of people don't think a Black and White couple looks right. People will make fun of them. I think they should stop being so friendly."
- "Most people don't see anything wrong with a mixed relationship as long as the two people are happy."
- "If the differences between a mixed couple can be worked out, then they are just like any other couple."

Solutions

- Elaine and John should get to know each other better before continuing their relationship.
- Elaine and John should speak to other interracial couples, their parents, and/or a health professional so that they can understand possible problems that might develop in their relationship.
- If Elaine and John are happy with each other, their relationship should continue.

Sample Paragraphs

Elaine has fallen for a new Black student, John, who transferred from another country. She thinks he is attractive and is fascinated by his accent and background. She has invited John to her home. Delores explains differences in their lifestyles in an effort to get Elaine to be objective.

A lot of people don't think a Black and White couple looks right. Most people don't see anything wrong with a mixed relationship as long as the two people are happy. Elaine and John should speak to other interracial couples, their parents, and/or a health professional so that they can understand possible problems that might develop in their relationship. If Elaine and John are happy with each other, then their relationship should continue.

"There Isn't Enough Time in My Day"

Discussion

Young teens have many responsibilities. These grow in number and difficulty as the teen grows older, and they more time to complete as they add up. Young teens have larger homework assignments, more studying to do, additional tests, class projects, sports practices and games, and other extracurricular activities to try. Young teens also have a new horizon to deal with as they are now socializing for the first time. This can include dating, parties, gatherings at school, and hanging out at friends' houses.

In addition, the older a teen gets, the more responsibilities he or she is given at home. Adults seem to feel that when a child enters the teen years, he or she becomes an adult and can be given full adult responsibilities. Teens are expected to complete all school assignments, keep their rooms clean, take care of younger siblings, manage their finances, participate in sports, join in family activities, and do well in school. All these time-consuming tasks loaded on to a child who is turning the corner to adulthood create tremendous frustration. In effect, a child's primary job, which is to do well in school, is now added to a second job of fulfilling family obligations. The pressure encountered can cause symptoms of anxiety and depression, which can lead to a loss of interest in many of these tasks.

Where can teens find the time to do what is expected? This issue makes it necessary to establish time management skills, but are young teens ready to accept these requirements? The National Institute of Mental Health indicates that 17.3 million Americans have suffered at least one major depressive episode. If 7.1 percent of adults have difficulty with everyday tasks, then we can assume that the numbers would be the same for children turning into adults. In fact, according to the Centers for Disease Control and Prevention, 7.1 percent of children in the United States have been diagnosed with anxiety. In addition, 1.9 million children in the US suffer from depression.

In the following script, we see two young teens discussing the problems of being treated like adults before their time:

Script

NEAL   Hi, Sally. Did you hear about the party that Sam is throwing on Sunday?

SALLY   Yes, I got a message on my phone, but I can't go. My parents are going out and I have to babysit. Besides, I have to study for the test we are having on Monday.

NEAL   I'm going to study on Saturday. My parents wanted me to go to my cousin's birthday party on Sunday, but I told them that I had to study for a test on Monday. When they leave, I'll head over to Sam's house.

SALLY   Do you think Marcia will be there?

NEAL   No way. Have you noticed how irritable she has become lately? She yells at you if you say something she doesn't like. And the other day I saw her crying in the cafeteria. That girl needs help to calm her down.

SALLY   I know. I try to stay away from her. By the way, when do you think you and I can work on our science project?

NEAL   When are you available?

SALLY   Can we meet after school on Monday?

NEAL   I can't. I have basketball practice. What about Tuesday?

SALLY   On Tuesday I'm meeting Joan to work on our history report. What about Wednesday?

NEAL   I'm good for Wednesday. We can walk to the library together and finish off the report about last week's experiment.

SALLY   Good. The report is due on Friday. I'll do my English paper Monday while you are at basketball practice.

NEAL   Are your parents busting your chops about cleaning the house?

SALLY   Because my siblings destroy the living room every day, my mother cleans it. I am only responsible for my bedroom. I usually clean it before I leave for school.

NEAL   I look forward to our meeting on Wednesday. I enjoy spending time with you. You are cute and funny. Maybe we can go a date when the holidays come.

SALLY   I like you too. It would be fun to spend time together if we ever finish our responsibilities. I wonder how our friends and classmates feel about their school and home jobs?

Problems

Neal and Sally are young teens with many new adult responsibilities. To deal with these extra responsibilities, they need to establish time management skills.

Parents feel that as soon as children turn to young teens, they can be treated as adults. They buy them cell phones and tablets, which take up a good deal of the teen's day.

All these extra duties can lead to anxiety and depression, which can cause teens to lose interest in many of these tasks.

Students spend too much time on their tablets and/or cell phones.

Comments

- "Many young teens feel that they work harder than their parents for no money. When they get an allowance, they must manage their money."

- "Young teens feel anxious and depressed when they can't complete tasks or they make mistakes."
- "Young teens don't have enough time in the day to handle all their tasks."

Solutions

- Parents need to understand that young teens have a major job keeping up with schoolwork. They must limit their jobs at home and make sure they get any help needed to be successful in school.
- Parents need to limit the hours that their young teens spend on their phones and tablets.
- Teachers need to monitor the work that children are assigned to complete. They should make individual adjustments to make sure that young teens experience success.
- Teachers need to monitor levels of frustration. If they see signs of anxiety or depression, they must make sure that the teen receives appropriate counseling when they see the child losing interest in tasks.

Sample Paragraphs

Neal and Sally are young teens with many new adult responsibilities. To deal with these extra responsibilities, they need to establish time management skills. Parents feel that as soon as children turn to young teens, they can be treated as adults. Young teens don't have enough time in their days to handle all their tasks. All these extra duties can lead to anxiety and depression, which can cause them to lose interest in many of these tasks. Parents need to understand that young teens have a major job keeping up with schoolwork. They must limit their jobs at home and make sure they get any help needed to be successful in school. Parents need to limit the hours that their young teens spend on their phones and tablets too.

Teachers need to monitor the work that children are assigned to complete. They should make individual adjustments to make sure that young teens experience success. Teachers need to monitor levels of frustration also. If they see signs of anxiety or depression, they must make sure that the teen receives appropriate counseling when they see the child losing interest in tasks.

SECTION III
GENERAL

"My House Stinks"

Objective

In this lesson, children will learn to deal with a problem that they did not create but cannot escape.

Statistics show that smoking among high school students is at the lowest level since 1991. Although cigarette smoking has decreased from 28 percent in 1991 to 11 percent in 2015, smoking is still a huge problem in the United States. One in five Americans still smokes some form of tobacco. Smoking not only affects those who do it, but often hurts those who are close to the smokers. Students who are subjected to secondhand smoke and who therefore suffer along with those who smoke deserve a better fate. The teacher should ask for comments from students who suffer along with parents or siblings who pollute their lungs and invade their space. If students do not respond, the teacher may use the following script to stimulate the conversation:

Script

JOHN   Hey, Sammy. How are you doing?

SAMMY   I have this nasty cough.

JOHN   What is that smell? It smells like smoke.

SAMMY   It is probably my clothes. My parents smoke in the house, and everything smells like smoke. My brothers and I are constantly coughing. We drink cough medicine like soda pop.

JOHN   Why don't you tell your parents to stop smoking? Can't they see that they are making you sick?

SAMMY   We told them many times, but they are addicted to nicotine and can't stop. It seems like every time my dad puts out a cigarette, my mom lights one up. Everything in the house smells from cigarette smoke, including our clothes and the drapes. Even our dog smells awful. I always volunteer to walk him so I can get some fresh air outside.

JOHN   My cousin's mother smokes. He was at war with his mother until she agreed to stop smoking in the house. Maybe you and your brothers can make a deal with your parents. Let's ask our classmates what they would do.

Problems

The house stinks because the student's parents smoke.

He and his brothers cough a lot because of secondhand smoke. The drapes, carpeting, and clothes all smell of smoke. The student can't even play with his dog because its coat stinks. Cigarettes are so expensive that the family has less food, fewer clothes and no family vacations.

The student and his brothers go to school smelling of smoke. He hates it when his parents kiss him good night because of the odor.

Comments

- "My parents don't smoke, but my uncle smokes cigars. I hate going to his house."
- "Tell your parents that smoking cigarettes can kill them. Smoking made my family sick."
- "My parents used to smoke, but the doctor gave them patches, which they used to help them stop."
- "When my parents quit smoking, we had extra money to eat out. When my parents quit smoking they had the whole house cleaned, and now we have no odors and we all are breathing better."
- "I hate being near people who smoke. I go outside whenever I see people light up."
- "My cousin smokes pot, and if you think cigarettes smell bad, you can't believe how bad that smells."

Solutions

- Teens should tell their parents that they need to stop smoking. Doctors say that smoking affects the health of the whole family.
- Teens should approach other family members who don't smoke and have them gang up on their parents.
- Teens should explore the internet to find articles to show their parents saying that they are harming themselves and everyone else in the house.
- Teens should encourage their parents to see a doctor for help to quit smoking.

Sample Paragraph

My house stinks because my parents smoke. Everything in our house smells of smoke. Everyone is always coughing because of the smell of smoke. Cigarettes are so expensive that there is less money for food, clothes, and vacations. If my parents quit smoking, there will be extra money to eat out. If my parents get patches, they can quit smoking. When my parents quit, we will all breathe better. Whenever I see people smoking indoors, I go outside where I can breathe better.

"What Do You Mean, Stay Away from Black People?"

Discussion

Our country is under attack. Our policing needs reform, African Americans are demanding equality, Democrats are fighting Republicans, people are not working because they have lost their jobs, and many people are depressed. We treat old friends like purveyors of disease. We bring food into our house instead of eating in a restaurant. We order online instead of going to stores. Our children sometimes do their studies at home. We stay away from people we see on the street. Most people are depressed. We are afraid to go out at night, we watch communities being hijacked, our schools are failing our children, and police and EMTs can't get to protest areas. The media constantly reminds us of how terrible things are. We see no end to fatal health problems. Politicians tell us they know best .

No one knows how others are suffering. They are only concerned with their own circumstances and are selfish with regard to others.

The following script illustrates the problem that a store owner encountered when "peaceful" demonstrators took over a section of her city. The owner had his store vandalized in one demonstration and looted in a second demonstration. Unfortunately, the entire family had to pay the price.

Script

LAURIE   Boy, have I had a terrible day.

SARAH   Why? What happened?

LAURIE   Have you heard about the "peaceful" protests going on in our city?

SARAH   Of course. The protestors have been roaming through all retail areas and helping themselves to anything they can steal. How does that affect you?

LAURIE   My father owns a store downtown. During last week's protest, someone threw a brick through my father's store window. When he got to the store the next morning, luckily nothing had been stolen. With the fear of more protests, he had the front of the store boarded up. Last night there was another "peaceful" protest. This time they had metal bars that they used to pull the boards down. They went into the store and stole everything that wasn't nailed down. My dad was completely wiped out.

SARAH   Didn't he have insurance?

LAURIE   Insurance only covers an act of nature or a fire that was caused by a mechanical malfunction. My father lost everything.

SARAH   Where were the police?

LAURIE   When they got to the scene, they were attacked by the protesters and had to leave the scene.

SARAH   Can't your father sue the city for failure to protect his property?

LAURIE   Are you kidding? The mayor said that the protesters were fighting for rights that they should have had a hundred years ago. He not only justified their actions but also criticized the police for inciting the protesters to do more damage. Those who attacked the police were taken to jail, and according to city policy, they were released the same night. I am sure that the thugs who broke my father's windows were right there the next night to put him out of business. The police have been told to stand down so they don't engage those who are doing the damage.

SARAH   I am so sorry that your family lost their business. What does your father plan to do now?

LAURIE   He plans to rebuild his business because there are no jobs to be had after COVID-19. Since there was no insurance money, he has to use all the money in my college fund.

SARAH   So, you will pay the price for the protests too. How unfair. I know a lot of people who are very upset with what is going on in this country. What did your friends say?

LAURIE   My Black friends say that it's about time. My White friends say that we are in for a war. My father says, "Stay away from Black people." I am lost.

Problems

Laurie's father had his business attacked twice. He lost everything.
Laurie's father had to use her college money to reopen his business.
People are allowed to destroy property and hurt others.
The police don't challenge those doing the damage and feel betrayed by many mayors who are reducing their numbers on the police force and telling them not to confront criminals. Many cities are firing school guards, and student safety is in question.

Comments

- "Many of my friends and family members are afraid to leave their houses after dark."
- "My father talks about getting a gun to protect the family."
- "I can understand that Black people feel discriminated against, but they don't have the right to attack others."
- "It is obvious that Black people cause police to use force against them, and when they are hurt, they accuse the police of brutality."
- "Without school security, we will all be targets for those who look for trouble."

Solutions

- Police need to protect people and businesses.
- The police force should not be limited or reduced during protests.
- Politics should not be allowed to affect crime and punishment.
- Cities should reimburse businesses that have been destroyed by illegal acts.
- Students should feel safe in their schools. By defunding police and limiting their powers, students will feel threatened.
- Police must be kept strong. Wherever numbers in the police force have been reduced, urban crime has gone way up. The police force should not be limited or reduced during protests.

Sample Paragraph

Laurie's father had his business attacked twice. He lost everything, and he had to use her college money to reopen his business. People are allowed to destroy property and hurt others. Many cities are firing school guards, causing student safety to be put into question. Without school security, we students will all be targets for those who look for trouble. Many of my friends and family members are afraid to leave their houses after dark. I can understand that Black people feel discriminated against, but they don't have the right to attack others. Police need to protect people and businesses. Their force should not be limited or reduced during protests. Police must be kept strong. Wherever police forces have been reduced, crime has gone way up.

"Food for Thought"

Discussion

To discuss hunger and emphasize the fact that there is no shame in being hungry and to discuss ways to get everyone fed, the teacher should be aware that the United States Department of Agriculture has determined that one out of every five American children goes to bed hungry. Many more have little or no food to eat over the weekend. Twenty-one million children get their only nutritious food at school.

Children must be made aware that there are resources for any students willing to discuss this problem, and the teacher should explain that there is no shame in being hungry. The teacher may explain that at certain times during the year, even teachers can find money scarce and might have to compromise their diet. In addition, parents often lose their jobs or have emergencies. The teacher may then launch into a discussion of how several of the children in class are probably affected by hunger and how we are all able to help in getting everyone fed. If children are still reluctant to discuss their individual issues, the following script may be used to begin the interaction:

Script

To defuse controversy about this subject, you will need three players to deliver the message.

JOSE   Good morning, John. How was your weekend?

JOHN   It was OK. I slept most of Saturday and watched TV on Sunday. What did you do?

JOSE   My friends and I went bike riding Saturday, and my family went out to dinner on Sunday.

JOHN   Elvin, are you eating your breakfast? I didn't have time to eat this morning.

ELVIN   It's all yours. My mom made me eggs and toast before I came to school.

JOSE   You can have mine too. I had a bag of chips on my way to school.

JOHN   Thanks. I am really hungry this morning.

ELVIN   John, didn't you ask me for my fish sandwich at lunch on Friday?

JOSE   I gave you mine too. What's with all the food, John?

JOHN   My brother is too young for school, and he eats amazing amounts of food. He loved the fish sandwiches.

JOSE   John, you are the one who ate the three boxes of cereal this morning. Is there a problem with food at home?

ELVIN   When my dad lost his job last year, my sister and I went to sleep without supper and went to our grandmother's for food on the weekends. It took nearly a month for Dad to find a new job and put food back on the table.

JOSE   My best friend had the same problem. He would tell me that he got awful headaches, and when there was no food, he felt like he had to vomit, but nothing would come out. Even after having breakfast in school, his teacher said he fell asleep at his desk. His parents looked for help and found a lot of places that were able to give them food.

ELVIN   I'm sure the kids in the class can bring in food without knowing who it's for. You can wait until school lets out and then take it home with you.

JOHN   Since I go on the bus, that won't work. Maybe the teacher and the other students have some ideas. If I bring it up, everyone will know I have a problem. Could you guys talk to the teacher?

JOSE   Sure. I could tell her about my friend and ask her to talk about all the hungry kids who have little to eat.

ELVIN   I'll help. Now that we have food again, I can tell my story.

JOHN   Thanks, guys. I'm glad you are my friends.

Problems

Many children do not have enough food to eat. Some may get all their food from school. When children don't have enough to eat, they can get sick. No one wants to talk about not having enough food, because it is embarrassing.

Comments

- "Schools should be open on Saturday and Sunday for feeding hungry students."
- "Parents should try to get money from other family members."
- "Students should seek ways to help other students who need more food."

Solutions

- Agencies that provide food for hungry families include Food for the Poor, Feeding America, and Project Open Hand. These agencies and others have food pantries in many areas.
- The hungry student can try to get food from other family members.
- Schools should raise money for the agencies so that all kids who need food can get it.
- The teacher should make sure that everyone knows about the problem and should tell students that no one should be embarrassed if they need help.

Sample Paragraph

Many children do not have enough food to eat. Children who don't have enough to eat can get very sick. Teachers need to tell students not to be embarrassed if there is no food at home, because help is available. We need to get food for these children. Parents have to ask relatives for food and money. Students have to help their friends to get food. Hungry families need to locate food pantries and agencies that can give them food. Students can help raise money for the agencies that can feed their friends.

Loneliness = Hurting

Objective

At one time or another, students may feel abandoned. Parents may go on vacation, leaving the child with a relative; a child may be shipped off to a relative for the summer; or the child may not do well on a task and exile himself or herself from the world around him or her. If bullied, a child may feel that the whole world is against him or her and may feel alone in the world. In any event, feeling alone can hurt. Statistics show that children who are lonely are 26 percent more likely to hurt themselves than students who receive support from others. Students can be lonely even when surrounded by hundreds of other students. Professionals need to identify these students and make sure they get help.

The professional should introduce the events descried in the first paragraph and ask if children have ever felt alone in the world. The professional should explain that feeling alone is not unusual but can lead to self-esteem problems, which affect how children feel and perform. Professionals must be able to suggest how children can find friendship and offer alternatives to being lonely, such as getting help from the school psychologist.

If there is no spontaneous discussion, the leader may want to use the following script. Remember, the script should be the last resort.

Script

ALLISON   Wasn't summer school awful?

MARIA   It was worse than awful. I hated it. It ruined my whole day. We got tons of homework, and there was no one to talk to. I was miserable.

ALLISON   There were a hundred students taking classes. Didn't you have any friends to study with?

MARIA   There were only a few kids from my class in our grade, and the rest were from different classes. What's worse is that my best friend was not here.

ALLISON   Why not?

MARIA   Felicia went to Puerto Rico. Both her parents work, so she went to her grandmother's for the summer. Her grades were better than mine, so she wasn't required to attend summer school. I was lost without her. She was the only one I could talk to.

ALLISON   What about your parents?

MARIA   They both work and don't get home until six o'clock in the evening. When I got home, I was alone all afternoon. Even when they called, they couldn't talk for more than a minute. I can't believe how lonely it got without Felicia. She lives in my building, and we were together every day. Sometimes my parents had to send her home because it was our bedtime.

ALLISON   You sound depressed. Couldn't you have picked another friend to spend time with?

MARIA   The friends who went to summer school all live too far away. There was no one to walk them home.

ALLISON   I think you were hurting and should have talked to someone about your loneliness. Let's ask our classmates how they feel about what happened.

Problems

Summer school was awful.
Maria hated it because it ruined her whole day, she had a great deal of homework, and she was alone most of the day.
Maria was also lonely because her best friend was away.
The students in Maria's summer school class lived too far away to get together with her.

Comments

- "My parents got me help in math so I wouldn't have to go to summer school. After summer school classes ended, Maria could have attended a summer day camp. That would have kept her busy during the afternoon and after summer school ended."
- "Maria's parents could have gotten her a dog or cat to help make her less lonely."
- "Maria could have talked to the guidance counselor to help her with her loneliness."

Solutions

- Maria should make sure to do her work during the year so she won't have to go to summer school again.
- Maria could have called Felicia every day since calls to Puerto Rico are free from the United States.
- If Felicia doesn't go to summer school next year, perhaps Maria could go with her to Puerto Rico. (Her parents can pay for her food.) A dog or cat would make her less lonely.
- Maria should talk to a professional to see if she is depressed or in need of counseling.

Sample Paragraph

Maria hated summer school because it ruined her day and she had to do a lot of homework. Her best friend was away, and she had no one to talk to. The best solution is for Maria to get help so that she doesn't have to go to summer school next year. If Maria has to go, she could attend a day camp that would help with her loneliness. A dog or cat could also help Maria to deal with her loneliness. Maria might go to Puerto Rico with her friend next summer. She should talk to a professional to see if she needs counseling.

"Whom Do I Choose?"

Objective

According to the CDC (Centers for Disease Control and Prevention), one out of two marriages in the United States ends in divorce. The good news is that in recent years, divorces have declined by 18 percent. The bad news is that fewer couples are getting married and are just living together and having children out of wedlock.

It is therefore inevitable that some students will be caught in the middle of a separation battle and may be forced to choose between their parents. This can be devastating to young teens, who are forming their own opinions about marriage and relationships. The following script illustrates a situation that young teens may be forced to endure:

Script

JOYCE   Lana, you look so sad. Were you crying? What is wrong?

LANA   My mother and father had a terrible fight. They screamed at each other for an hour, and then Dad left the house.

JOYCE   My parents fight and yell at each other once a week. Dad leaves the house, has a few drinks, and then comes home to sleep.

LANA   My parents have fought in the past, but this time Dad said he wanted a divorce. He stormed out of the house and didn't come back.

JOYCE   Where do you think he went?

LANA   Mom said she called his mother and that is where he slept.

JOYCE   Did he take his clothes?

LANA   His mother said she tried to talk him into going home. She also said he would pick up his clothes today. She told my mom to pack his things.

JOYCE   It sounds serious. Do you think he'll go through with it?

LANA   I don't know, but I love both my parents and I don't want to see them split.

JOYCE   I don't blame you. What did they fight about?

LANA   Mom says there isn't enough money for all of us to live on. Dad wants Mom to get a job. Mom said she wants to be a stay-at-home mom until we are old enough to take care of ourselves. She wants Dad to ask for a raise.

JOYCE   How do you feel about your mom getting a job?

LANA   I can take care of myself, but my younger brothers and sister still need Mom around. They can't do anything without Mom giving them directions.

JOYCE   My parents always fight about money. Mom smokes, and Dad drinks. If they both quit, we'd be rich. Neither of those things will happen anytime soon.

LANA   At least your parents realize the situation and stay together. My dad wants out, and that would be a disaster.

JOYCE   What will you do if they do split?

LANA   I would have to stay with Mom to help with my siblings. If I went with Dad, I'd have to change my school, and I'd be abandoning my family.

JOYCE   I agree, but I would do everything I could to get them back together. I wonder what our classmates would do.

Problems

Lana's parents are fighting, and her father wants a divorce.

They are fighting because they don't have enough money. Lana don't want to have to choose between them.

Comments

- "My parents fight over money, but they stay together."
- "Our family would be destroyed if our parents split."
- "If money is an issue, why are the parents smoking and drinking?"
- "Why do parents have to fight?"
- "Are children the reason for parents fighting?"

Solutions

- Get the family together and have the teen talk to the parents.
- The parents need to see a marriage counselor.
- Tell Mom to get a part-time job so that she gets home when the kids get home from school.
- If Grandmother is available, she can watch the kids while Mom goes to work.
- The parents need to quit smoking and drinking to see how much more money would be available.
- The kids could help around the house so Mom is free to get a job.

Sample Paragraphs

Parents fight about not having enough money. Students usually don't want them to fight, to divorce, or to leave the family. They don't want to have to choose between them. If the parents split, the family will be destroyed. The parents should stop drinking and smoking so there is more money for the family.

The rest of the family and a marriage counselor need to help the parents to stay together. The mom needs to get a part-time job to bring in more money, and perhaps a grandmother can watch the kids while the mom works.

"That Dress Looks Great on You"

Objective

Many families in our country are living below the poverty level. This situation impacts schoolchildren of parents who are struggling to make ends meet. The following scenario illustrates how children are affected and shows that they should not lose hope that things will get better:

Script

TAMIKA   Hi, Haley. How are you?

HALEY   I'm OK.

TAMIKA   Are you sure? You don't sound OK. What's wrong?

HALEY   I'll be fine.

TAMIKA   Maybe going to Jake's birthday party on Saturday will cheer you up.

HALEY   I'm not going.

TAMIKA   Why not? Jake said he wanted the whole class to come to his party.

HALEY   l have nothing to wear. And I won't go in my school clothes.

TAMIKA   You don't have a dress that you can wear?

HALEY   Both my parents lost their jobs and are looking for work. There is no money for clothes in my family. I've outgrown everything I had and gave all my clothes to my younger sister. I'm glad we have food on the table. Dad is taking odd jobs, and Mom is cleaning houses to earn some money to feed us.

TAMIKA   l know how you feel. My parents were out of work two years ago. I had no new clothes for a long time. They both got jobs, and we are all doing well now. Why don't you come over to my house Saturday morning and we'll do our homework together?

HALEY   Are you sure it will be OK with your mother?

TAMIKA   Sure. She likes when my friends come over.

(Saturday morning at Tamika's house.)

TAMIKA   Haley, I'm glad you came.

HALEY   Thanks for inviting me. My siblings can drive me nuts on the weekends.

TAMIKA   So can mine. We'll do our homework later, but I want to show you something. (*Goes to her closet and takes out a dress.*) What do you think about this dress? When my parents went back to work, my mom took me shopping and bought it for me. It looks beautiful, but it doesn't fit me right. I wonder how it would look on you. I think you should go into the bathroom and try it on.

HALEY   Why? If it doesn't fit you, it probably won't fit me.

TAMIKA   Let's see. It will only take a minute. I'd like to see it on you.

HALEY   I'm not sure it's the right thing to do. Your mom might get upset.

TAMIKA   Mom won't even know. Please. I just want to see how it looks on someone else.

HALEY   OK. But just for one minute. I'll be right out. (*Puts on the dress and returns to the room.*)

TAMIKA   That dress looks great on you.

HALEY   It does fit well, and it is a beautiful dress. Thank you for letting me try it on.

TAMIKA   Leave it on a minute. I want my mom to see it.

HALEY   No. She'll get upset if she sees me wearing your clothes.

TAMIKA   No she won't. She knows it doesn't fit me. While you were trying it on, she told me that if it fits you, you should take it home. She was going to donate it to the thrift store. She would love to see it put to good use by my friend. In fact, she is calling your mom right now to tell her that we would love to see you wearing it.

HALEY   I don't know what to say. I love it.

TAMIKA   Say you'll wear it to Jake's birthday party, because I'm going to call him to say you are coming.

HALEY   Do you think I can go?

TAMIKA   Of course. He told us he wanted the entire class to come to his party.

Problems

Many families have little or no money to spend on clothes. This affects students going to school and may cause them to miss events or be embarrassed.

Comments

- "Some parents might ask other relatives to loan them some money until they can get a job."
- "Many parents shop in thrift stores, where they get great clothes for less money. There are thrift stores all over the city."

- "When I outgrow my clothes, I give them to my siblings, so they last for many years."
- "If students don't have younger brothers or sisters, they can donate their clothes to thrift organizations so they can be reused."

Solutions

- Students should share whatever they can with their friends and relatives.
- Everyone should be aware of places where they can get items they need at reduced prices.
- If students have clothes or other items they no longer need, they should donate them to the school's clothing drive or stores that can resell them to others at cheap prices.

Sample Paragraph

Many families that have little or no money to spend on clothes. This affects students going to school and may cause them to miss events or be embarrassed. Students should share whatever they can with their friends and relatives. When I outgrow my clothes, I give them to my siblings, so they last for many years. Many parents shop in thrift stores, where they get great clothes for less money. If students have clothes or other items they no longer need, they should donate them to the school's clothing drive and stores that can resell them to others at cheap prices.

"What Is a Picture Worth?"

Objective

In the previous story, Tamika gave Haley a dress so she could feel good about going to Jake's birthday party. Haley was as happy as she could be until a picture ruined everything. (Note that for the following role-play, this time two different students should be chosen to represent Haley and Tamika.)

Script

HALEY   Wasn't Jake's party amazing? I had the best time—a better time than I have had in forever. Thank you again for that beautiful dress. Without it, I would never have gone to the party.

TAMIKA   I had a great time too. Unfortunately, things didn't work out as well as I'd hoped.

HALEY   What do you mean?

TAMIKA   Remember when Jake blew out all the candles on his cake and told us his wish was to have all the girls at the party kiss him?

HALEY   Yes. All the girls kissed him on the cheek. What was wrong with that?

TAMIKA   It seems that Jamal had his older brother's phone so he could call home to be picked up when the party ended. He used that phone to take a picture of you kissing Jake.

HALEY   You're kidding, right?

TAMIKA   I wish I was. Jamal was showing your picture to everyone in the cafeteria at breakfast.

HALEY   If my mother finds out, I'll never be allowed to go to a party again. If one of the kids tells their mother and then she tells my mother at a PTO meeting, I'm toast. And what if his older brother posts the picture on social media? I'll be grounded for life.

TAMIKA   Find Jamal and see if he will delete the picture from his brother's phone.

HALEY   Why would he? If he is showing it to everyone, he obviously feels it is a gossip item. I can confront him, but that might make him even more determined to embarrass me.

TAMIKA   You're probably right. I think you should tell your mother before she hears it from someone else. Tell her that all the girls kissed Jake on the cheek, but one student took a picture of you.

HALEY   What if Jamal uses the picture against me with our classmates?

TAMIKA   I'll make sure that all the girls who were at the party realize that they could be in your shoes and that they need to support you.

Problems

Haley feels that she is in trouble because Jamal took a picture of her kissing Jake. Jamal has been showing the picture of Haley kissing Jake to everyone in the cafeteria.

Haley's picture is on Jamal's brother's phone and can be posted on social media.

If Haley's mother finds out, she might ground Haley.

Comments

- "Haley is in trouble. Her mother is going to ground her."
- "Jamal should not have taken a picture of Haley kissing Jake. It should be erased from his brother's phone."
- "Haley should go to the principal and have the picture erased from Jamal's phone."
- "Haley needs to tell her mother what happened."
- "All the girls in the class need to tell the teacher that Haley didn't do anything wrong."

Solutions

- Haley must tell her mother and the teacher what happened at the party.
- The girls who were there must support Haley so everyone knows she did nothing wrong.
- Jamal must bring his brother's phone to school so that the picture of Haley can be deleted.
- The teacher must caution the students about taking pictures of others without their permission. He or she must also explain the damage that can be done if a picture reaches social media.
- Jamal should apologize to Haley for showing her picture around the cafeteria.

Sample Paragraph

Haley had a great time at Jake's party, but now she feels that she is in trouble because Jamal took a picture of her kissing Jake. If Haley's mother finds out, she might ground Haley. Jamal should not have taken a picture of Haley kissing Jake. It should be erased from his brother's phone. Haley needs to tell her mother and the teacher what happened. All the girls in the class need to tell the teacher that Haley didn't do anything wrong. Jamal must bring his brother's phone to school so that the picture can be deleted. The teacher must caution the students about taking pictures of others without their permission. He or she must also explain the damage that can be done if a picture reaches social media.

"I Didn't Sleep Last Night"

Objective

Older students love their siblings. They are fun to play with take care of and help keep the family together. There are times, however, when younger siblings can be a burden and actually cause the functioning of older siblings to suffer.

Script

LARRY   Hey, Willy, you look exhausted. What happened?

WILLY   I can hardly keep my eyes open. I fell asleep at my desk during our art period. The teacher told the class to let me sleep.

LARRY   What happened to make you so tired?

WILLY   My little sister was sick last night and couldn't stop crying. She cried for hours.

LARRY   What was wrong with her?

WILLY   My parents thought she had a stomach virus. She was in terrible pain, and nothing helped to stop her crying. We live in a small apartment, so there was no way for any of us to get any sleep. During the night, my mother called the doctor and left a message that she would bring my sister in first thing in the morning. The problem was that we couldn't get her to stop crying. At one point Dad wanted to take her to the hospital, but she calmed down for a few minutes, so we really didn't know how serious it was.

LARRY   We have a science test in an hour. Did you study?

WILLY   I tried, but I couldn't concentrate because I felt bad for my sister. My other siblings were upset, and no one was able to do homework or study. My problem will be staying awake and concentrating during the test.

LARRY   This test is going to be hard. I studied long and hard and still had trouble understanding several concepts. Why don't you talk to the teacher and see if she can give you the test at a different time?

WILLY   Would that be fair to the other students?

LARRY   We all have problems like yours at one time or another. As long as you promise not to talk to anyone about the test, maybe the teacher can give you the test when we have our prep period tomorrow.

WILLY   I don't know if I will be ready. I am really concerned about what is wrong with my sister. I hope she is all right.

LARRY   When my sister cried all night, she was teething and was fine the next day.

Problems

Willy was kept awake all night by his crying sister.

Willy's parents need to prevent this from happening again? Willy couldn't study for his science test because he was worried about his sister.

Perhaps Willy's teacher give him a makeup test. If he or she does, then the other students may try to take advantage. The teacher should consider his or her options. Willy's parents should determine what they can do to help their son.

Comments

- "Willy's parents should have taken the baby to the hospital when she wouldn't stop crying."
- "The teacher should give Willy a makeup test."
- "The teacher should call Willy's parents to confirm the problem."
- "The teacher should not count Willy's grade for this test."
- "The teacher should not have to give a makeup test."
- "Maybe Willy will do well because he attended class every day."
- "If Willy gets a makeup test, all students should get the same deal."

Solutions

- The teacher should make a note next to Willy's grade if his score is lower than expected.
- Willy's parents should make sure that if the problem happens again, they will have a plan to get help for the baby.
- Willy's mom should call the teacher to explain what happened and ask the teacher to help Willy with his problem.

Sample Paragraph

Willy was kept awake all night because his sister was crying. He couldn't study for his science test because he was worried about his sister. Willy's parents should have taken his sister to the hospital when she wouldn't stop crying. Willy's mom should have called the teacher to explain what happened and ask the teacher to help Willy with his problem. The teacher should make a note next to Willy's grade if his score is lower than expected. Willy's parents should make sure that if the problem happens again, they have a plan to get help for the baby.

"Hey, What about Me?"

Discussion

Some families are growing. It is not unusual for students to be members of large families. There are times when siblings love each other and times when they become jealous of each other. Most times the intention is not to cause jealousy, but still it can take its toll on a sibling who feels that he or she is being ignored. Going through puberty can exacerbate the situation. Increased attention to certain members of a family can leave young teens with feelings of anxiety and insecurity. They may feel isolated and disconnected and may lapse into depression. When these signs appear, it is everyone's responsibility to make the teen whole again.

The effort must begin with other family members. Parents must recognize that they are favoring certain children over others and equalize the attention they give to all their children. They must then encourage other family members to follow suit and pay equal attention to all siblings. They must also monitor all siblings to make sure that they are aware of jealousies. Teachers must avoid establishing teacher's pets and must monitor classroom remarks among the students. It is naive to think that other students will not favor some classmates. It is the teacher's responsibility to level the playing field by showing extra attention to those who are shunned by their peers.

In the following script, we see students discussing favoritism toward one student's twin sisters. It is important to note the jealousy of David and to realize that his problem is a serious one.

Script

SEAN   l am glad we got together over the weekend. Your twin baby sisters are so cute. I loved playing with them. How old are they now?

DAVID   They just turned four years old, and I love them so much.

SEAN   You are so lucky.

DAVID   Not really. Sometimes my parents seem to forget I'm their son.

SEAN   What do you mean?

DAVID   Sometimes I feel like I'm not a member of the family. When my mother takes us shopping, she only looks for clothes for the twins or my older brother. I get hand-me-downs from my brother and never get anything new for myself. Mom treats the twins like movie stars, whereas I feel like an afterthought. If I'm doing homework when the twins get hungry, Mom takes them to a fast-food restaurant while I get tuna or peanut butter when she gets home. Daddy's little girls could set the house on fire and it would be all right with him The twins get more toys in a month than I had in all my years growing up. My grandparents ignore me and my brother and play with the twins for hours. I don't even know why we have to go to their house. My brother and I work hard to get good grades, but my parents can't stop talking about how well the twins are doing in kindergarten.

SEAN   Wow, you are sure jealous of your sisters. From what you've said, I can't say I blame you. My cousin has several brothers and sisters and has complained about being ignored. How does your brother feel about the special treatment your sisters get?

DAVID   He loves them as much as I do. Being the oldest, he gets new clothes and is old enough to be on his own a lot. He also gets an allowance, which lets him get some extra food. He is not as angry as I am.

SEAN   Have you told your parents how you feel?

DAVID   I complained when they took the twins shopping, but they still treat them like superstars.

SEAN   Obviously, someone needs to plead your case. It would be my guess that support should come from other family members. You should be expressing your concerns to your grandparents and aunts and uncles. Adults could plead your case better than you could.

Problems

David is jealous of his younger twin sisters.
His sisters and older brother get new clothes, while he has to wear hand-me-downs.
His sisters get lots of toys, and they get fast food when they are hungry.
The twins get all kinds of attention from David's parents and grandparents. His brother is older and gets an allowance. Because of this, David's older brother is less jealous of the twins.
Many students who have siblings can relate to David's jealousy.

Comments

- "I am often annoyed when my brother gets special gifts because his grades are better than mine."
- "My parents ask me to babysit for my younger sister. It annoys me because she always wants to play when I have other things to do."
- "David needs to tell his parents that he is angry because the twins get everything."

Solutions

- David needs to admit he is jealous of his sisters.
- David needs to express his jealousy to all family members.
- David's parents need to admit that the twins get more attention than he and his brother get.

- David's parents need to take steps to equalize their attention and spending habits so that their four children feel equally loved.
- All parents, and even teachers, have favorites. Learning to control emotions is important to being successful in relationships.

Sample Paragraph

David is jealous of his twin sisters. His sisters and older brother get new clothes, whereas he has to wear hand-me-downs. The twins get all kinds of attention from the parents and grandparents. David needs to tell his parents that he is angry because the twins get everything. He also needs to admit that he is jealous of his sisters. David's parents need to take steps to equalize their attention and spending habits so that their four children feel equally loved. Learning to control emotions is important to being successful in relationships.

"Is Our School Safe?"

Objective

Given the many recent school shootings, every student has the right to ask if they will be safe when they enter their school. Parents and professionals must ask the same question. At the time of this writing in September 2024, there have been thirty school shootings around the country. Despite the many steps being taken to improve security on every campus, every student must wonder if his or her school will be next. This psychological mindset creates fear that students must live with each time they go through the school entrance.

Professionals should have little trouble encouraging students to discuss this topic. The professional's job is to deal with the psychological fears that students may express during conversations. The professional should be briefed on school safety issues and on how to deal with the many statements that might arise from students. Even if a school has never been attacked, students who watch media reports must be aware of signs of an attack. Professionals have to be aware of any triggers that can cause panic, including an unannounced fire drill, a car backfiring, a door slamming, or perhaps a threat made by an irate student. When one of these signs surfaces, the professional must begin the healing process. A teacher as the professional would have to take control of the class in an effort to get learning back to normal. (Instead of having students work individually, the teacher should create group among the comfort by reading aloud and working with the students.)

It would probably be wise to have the school psychologist present at the time of these lessons so that comments can be analyzed and any mental health problems can be identified. The professional should also be present at the parents' meeting about this topic so that concerns can be discussed and information disseminated.

If student communication falters or heads in the wrong direction, the following script may be assigned:

Script

Sam   Hi, Charlie. What's going on?

Charlie   I'm not sure. Have you spoken to Larry lately?

Sam   We had lunch together a couple of days ago. Why do you ask?

Charlie   I was talking to him an hour ago, and he seemed very angry. I asked if anything was wrong, and he started ranting about the lack of security in our school. I told him that we had a security agent and that we are all aware of what to do in an emergency. He told me that the security guard is an idiot who couldn't stop a dog from barking. He said that no one ever sees our guard and that a student could go through the metal detector and go right to an open window, where a friend could hand him a gun. He complained that no one cares about us and that after so many school shootings, the students here are sitting ducks. He said he doesn't understand why there aren't more mass shootings.

SAM   That doesn't sound good. What did you tell him?

CHARLIE   I told him he shouldn't be saying those things. I told him he could get into trouble if he told that to the wrong person. He said he didn't care. He said he was fed up with coming to school not knowing if he would be going home. He said he is not happy in school anyway as his grades are not good. He claimed that the teachers suck and don't understand him.

SAM   Do you think he could be a problem? Do you think we need to do something?

CHARLIE   I was thinking of saying something, but I didn't know if I should or who I should talk to. What do you think?

SAM   I think there is cause for concern. If you don't tell anybody and Larry flips out, you'll feel horrible.

CHARLIE   But if I get him in trouble, he'll be pissed at me.

SAM   But if you don't say anything and he snaps, you could be the first one he goes after.

CHARLIE   You're right. But who should I talk to? I don't want to go to the police.

SAM   You don't have to. You can tell your story to the guidance counselor or the teacher. If they feel there is a threat, they will take it to the proper authorities.

CHARLIE   I don't want to go alone. Would you go with me?

SAM   I'll go with you as long as you tell the same story you told me.

Problems

The problem is that to keep our schools safe, we need to know what safety procedures are in place.

Students need to know whom they can talk to if they suspect something is wrong.

We must focus on how to make our schools safer.

Comments

- "Gun control should make it harder to get guns."
- "We need to identify students who might present a problem."
- "We need to know what to do if there is an attack."
- "We need to know who to talk to if we feel there is danger."
- "I have nightmares thinking that we may be attacked."

Solutions

- We must do everything possible to keep our schools safe.
- Students must be aware of everything around them.
- If a student hears of a threat or sees a nasty change in another student's behavior, he or she must report it to the teacher, a guidance counselor, or the police.
- Students must discuss their fears with their friends and professionals. Students must seek help if they are afraid.

Sample Paragraph

We need to keep our schools safe. We need to know what to do if there is an attack. We need to identify students who might present problems. We need to know whom to talk to if we feel we are in danger or are afraid. We must be aware of what is going on around us. If we hear a threat or see a change in a student's behavior, we must report it to the teacher, a guidance counselor, or the police.

Objective

Addiction is a major problem all across the world. The effects of using drugs or alcohol are not limited to the user. Those who are close to substance abusers are also negatively affected. Young teens not only have to deal with the pressures exerted by their peers, but also often have to deal with the actions of their parents. This lesson deals with addiction and its effects. Obviously the addicted party cannot serve as the leader. A medical professional or an uninvolved relative can serve to initiate the discussion.

Addictions cause many different types of behavior. Drugs can make a person passive, extremely active, or even violent. Alcohol addiction can yield various reactions too. The natural reaction of loved ones is to deny there is a problem and try to lead normal lives. This philosophy can work as long as outsiders don't interfere with family life.

A drug or alcohol addiction could cause a severe reduction in household income. This affects everyone living in the house but can be particularly hard on young teens, who might not be able to get new clothes or school supplies as a result. It might even explain why one in five children goes to sleep hungry. An even tougher side effect of addiction is the guilt that close relatives may feel. Spouses, children, and parents may all blame themselves when problems arise. Young teens may blame themselves for an elder who does the wrong thing. This can lead to denial, depression, and even withdrawal.

When others become involved with the family, the chance of discovery of the problem can cause panic among family members. The need to hide the problem becomes paramount. Denial and avoidance are primary defense mechanisms that can lead to psychological problems.

There are many topics of discussion that can be pursued here. It is hoped that helpful discussions will begin solving problems. If the teen is reluctant to discuss the problems of addiction, then the leader may initiate a conversation by using the following script:

Script

STACY   Hey, June, isn't it great that we were assigned to work on the social studies project together? As best friends, it will be easy and fun for us. One day we can work at my house and the next at yours. When we finish for the day, we can listen to music or play video games.

JUNE   You know we can probably get more work done at the library. That way we can get the report done quickly and be done with it.

STACY   That's true, but we can't listen to music or have snacks there. We can have much more fun at each other's houses.

JUNE   True. But sometimes my dad is home, and I wouldn't want to disturb him.

STACY   We won't disturb him if we work in your room.

JUNE   We can't work in my apartment.

STACY   Why not? What's wrong in your apartment? Are your parents in trouble?

JUNE   If I tell you, you must swear not to tell anyone.

STACY   I promise. What's wrong?

JUNE   My dad has a drinking problem. He started drinking when he lost his job. When I get home from school, he is often drunk on the couch.

STACY   Has he ever hurt you or your sister?

JUNE   No. My mother would throw him out of house if he ever hurt us. He just wants us to go to our rooms. He doesn't want us to bother him, and he doesn't want us to bring anyone to the house.

STACY   What does your mother say?

JUNE   She is angry with him. She had to get a job to help us financially, and she yells at him every day that he gets drunk. She makes money, and he spends it on alcohol.

STACY   Has your mother tried to get him help?

JUNE   She has discussed it with our relatives. I heard them say that Dad has to see a doctor and a psychologist to get him into a program that will help him stop drinking. They have all pledged to help in any way possible. His sister even offered to let Dad move in with her family if he felt that would help him get better.

STACY   Do you think he will move out?

JUNE   We don't want him to live somewhere else, but we do want him to get help to stop drinking.

STACY   There is no reason for you to be punished. We can do the report at my house every day, and when we finish we can have snacks and listen to music.

Problems

June and Stacy cannot work on their report in June's apartment.

June's father is a drunk, and she does not want anyone to know about it. When June's father is drinking, he does not want anyone to visit the apartment.

June's father wants the children to stay in their rooms so they don't see him drinking.

June's mother had to get a job to help support the family because her father lost his job.

June's mother is very mad at her father because he is not working and spends the family's money on alcohol.

June doesn't know how to get her father help.

Comments

- "It is a shame that the girls cannot work in June's apartment."
- "It is nice that Stacy offered that they could do all their work in her apartment."
- "June's father has a problem, and he has to get help to solve it."
- "June's mother has to make sure that her husband gets help."
- "June must understand that her father has an addiction, and she must be sympathetic in encouraging him to get help."
- "June is lucky to have Stacy as a friend."
- "June is lucky that her family is willing to help her father beat his addiction."

Solutions

- June's family has to help her father deal with his addiction.
- June's father has to be willing to beat his addiction. He needs to see a doctor and get into a program that can help him.
- June must not feel guilty about her father's addiction. It is not her fault.
- June's mother must put her foot down and stop her husband's drinking.

Sample Paragraph

June's father is a drunk, and she doesn't want anyone to know about it. When he is drinking, he does not want anyone to visit the apartment. He wants his children to stay in their rooms so they don't see him drinking. June's mother had to get a job to support the family because June's father lost his job. It was nice of Stacy to offer her apartment so that the girls can get their report done. June must understand that her father has an addiction, and she must be sympathetic in encouraging him to get help. June is lucky that her family is willing to help her father beat his addiction. June's father needs to see a doctor and get into a program that can help him. June's mother must put her foot down to stop her husband's drinking.

Nobody Gets Hurt, so It Is All Right

Discussion

Shoplifting among young teens has become a sport. Stealing items from stores carries little, if any, punishment for those who are too young to be prosecuted. A principal from Chicago told me that some of his students played a game. During a given period, students would steal whatever they could, and the one with the items of greatest value would be declared the winner. Most business owners build losses into their inventories and are not interested in pressing charges against young teens. This does not justify or condone stealing, but time lost in prosecuting can cost them more than the items stolen.

A health professional must deal with this problem as a moral issue. Stealing is wrong on any level, and a successful theft can lead to bigger larcenies as teens get older. Discussions about what is right and wrong must be introduced to establish the correct pattern of behavior. Discussions should center on how students would feel if someone stole their backpack, jacket, or textbooks or other items that were important to them. A logical response would include, "The store owner is rich and won't miss the small item I took." The discussion should then explore how the store owner got started, and how hard he worked to earn his store and the merchandise that such a student feels is not important to him. The professional should then ask what is important to students and what they have to do to earn it. Then ask what would happen if they lost what they earned. This may include failing a test and losing a good grade, getting booted off a school team, or losing one's best friend because of a fight. Compare this to the disappointment of losing money that someone worked hard to get. The discussion might become more personal by asking how students would feel if someone stole their backpack or broke into their house and stole everything of value. It should be pointed out that stealing from a business is the same as stealing from a person's home. A business is part of a store owner's home.

Parents may not be aware that their children are involved in these activities, so the professional should involve parents in these conversations to add validity to the wrongdoing. This could be done by asking the parent of a guilty student to meet with them, or by holding a parents' meeting for all parents of a class with admitted shoplifters. The professional should also be prepared to deal with other moral issues that might be introduced into the lesson. Although the main thrust of the lesson is the discussion of shoplifting, topics such as cheating on tests, lying to others, not doing one's job properly, or deliberately hurting others to gain power might come up. These should not be ignored and might be suggested for other lessons. If students are reluctant to discuss things that they have done wrong, the following script may be used:

Script

EDDIE   Hi, Doug. What's going on?

DOUG   Not much. What's new with you?

EDDIE   That hat is cool. Where did you buy it?

DOUG   I got it at the department store.

EDDIE   How much did it cost?

DOUG   The price was right.

EDDIE   I'd like to get one. How much was it?

DOUG   I didn't pay for it. I took it.

EDDIE   You stole it? Why did you steal it?

DOUG   Students take things from all the stores around here. We cut the tags off and hide the things under our coats.

EDDIE   Aren't you afraid you'll get caught?

DOUG   It doesn't matter. All the stores have money set aside for theft. The managers don't want to spend the day in court, so they don't call the police. If we get caught, they take back the article and tell us not to come back to their store. If you like the hat, you can come with me on Saturday.

EDDIE   No, thanks. I think that stealing is wrong. Besides, if my parents found out, I'd be grounded for a month. Aren't your parents angry at you?

DOUG   They don't know. If they ask about something I took, I tell them I bought it with my allowance.

EDDIE   Wow. That is unbelievable.

DOUG   Not at all. There are gangs who take things every day. Some of our classmates are doing it, and they never get caught.

EDDIE   I would like to hear what our classmates have to say about shoplifting.

Problems

Shoplifting is a problem among young teens.

Stealing from stores is considered a fun sport rather than a violation of the law.

The fact that students are very young and that store owners are not likely to prosecute offenders makes teens more likely to take the risk.

Shoplifting may be a first step to other forms of immoral behavior.

Parents may not be aware that their children are stealing and should be involved in conversations about the practice.

Comments

- "My cousin was in a gang that used to take things from a department store. He used to give me some of the things they took."
- "My brother was caught cheating on a test and then lied to the teacher and my parents."
- "My friend was caught shoplifting by a security guard at the department store. My friend refused to give them his phone number, and the manager didn't call the police. He took back the stolen item and told my friend not to come back to the store."

Solutions

- The school must hold parent meetings to explain all the moral problems their children face.
- Parents should be encouraged to talk to students and teachers on a regular basis to prevent moral lapses.
- Store owners must be encouraged to increase security and to prosecute repeat offenders to discourage shoplifting.
- Professionals must discuss what is right and wrong in each classroom.
- Children must discuss and understand right from wrong.

Sample Paragraphs

Shoplifting is a problem among teens. The fact that students are very young and store owners are not likely to prosecute offenders makes teens more likely to take the risk. Shoplifting may be a first step to other forms of immoral behavior.

My cousin was in a gang that used to take things from a department store. He used to give me some of the things they took.

The school must hold parent meetings to explain all the moral problems their children face. Professionals must discuss what is right and wrong in each classroom. Children must discuss and understand right from wrong.

Discussion

Attitudes in the United States have changed. When I was growing up, if a person made a mistake, he or she followed it up by offering an apology and a way to make things right. Today's terminology consists of "l didn't do it" and "not guilty," regardless of the truth. Unfortunately, this attitude is not only seen by students in schools, but also is supported by parents. (When was the last time you heard someone charged with a crime plead guilty?)

I was once called to the principal's office, where I found the principal and a neighbor who lived down the street from the school. The man's house had been vandalized on Halloween, and he had a video showing the students and a cell phone that he had found in his bushes. He claimed that two windows were broken and his house was covered in eggs and toilet paper. He was upset but promised not to call the police if the boys agreed to clean the house. After viewing the tape, I was able to identify the students and made a list of their names. The principal called them to the office one at a time. When faced with dealing with the police, the first three agreed to clean the house. The fourth showed up with his mother the next day. The student absolutely denied involvement in the incident and told us that the video was wrong and that his three friends lied about his being there. His mother was adamant and kept saying that if her son said he was not there, then he wasn't there. The principal showed the mother the cell phone that had been found at the scene and asked her to dial her son's number. When the phone rang, she realized that her son was lying to her. With reluctance, she said that her son would help in the cleanup.

The following script indicates another problem that teens often face. Most students should have stories about classmates who deny things that they have done. If these stories don't yield desired results, then choose two students to role-play the following scenario:

Script

JOYCE   Althea, why are you crying?

ALTHEA   The teacher said I am in trouble and is calling for my parents to come to school.

JOYCE   What did you do?

ALTHEA   l didn't do anything. Madison brought her iPad to breakfast. She always reads her book while eating. When she went to hang her bag in the closet, she said the iPad was missing. The teacher asked everyone to open their book bags, and found Madison's iPad in my book bag.

JOYCE   How did it get there?

ALTHEA   l don't know. Someone must have put it there.

JOYCE   Why would someone put Madison's iPad in your book bag? If they wanted to steal it, they would have put it in their own bag.

ALTHEA   I know. That's why I can't figure out how it got into my bag.

JOYCE   What did the teacher say when you told her that someone else must have put it in your bag?

ALTHEA   She asked if anyone saw what happened. John said he saw me put it in my bag when Madison went up for milk.

JOYCE   Did you take the iPad? Don't you have your own?

ALTHEA   I don't have my own. My parents said I am too young and can't have my own until I get to middle school. All my friends have an iPad, and I am always looking over their shoulders and borrowing theirs.

JOYCE   So, you did take it. What will you do when your parents come up?

ALTHEA   I don't know. What would you do?

JOYCE   Since it's the first time you've been in trouble, if you admit to taking it and then apologize, chances are you'll just be told not to do it again. I doubt that you will be suspended. You'll probably need to promise you won't do it again. Let's ask our classmates how they would handle the situation.

Problems

In today's society, the phrase "I didn't do it" and claims of "not guilty" have become prevalent. People are not willing to admit that they have done anything wrong. Even when caught committing a wrong, most will deny it. What is worse, parents and friends who know the accused will often vouch for them and join in the denial.

People need to stop denying having done wrong when they are caught.

Someone knowledgeable should judge whether a crime has been committed.

Those who are caught doing wrong should be punished.

Comments

- "My brother told me that students were expelled from college for stealing answers to final exams. The students said they didn't do it but got thrown out anyway."
- "My parents told me to deny doing anything wrong and call them whenever I get into trouble."
- "My parents tell me that people who say they are innocent go to jail anyway when they are proven guilty."
- "My parents taught me that if I do something wrong, I should admit it and then apologize and promise I won't do it again."

Solutions

- Teachers and parents should teach children that honesty is the best policy.
- Teachers and parents should let children know that people make mistakes.
- If you make a mistake, you should admit it so the punishment will be less severe.
- When you make a mistake, you must correct it.

Sample Paragraphs

In today's society, the phrase "I didn't do it" and claims of "not guilty" have become prevalent. People are not willing to admit that they have done anything wrong. My parents tell me that people who say they are innocent go to jail anyway when they are proven guilty. My parents taught me that if I do something wrong, I should admit it and then apologize and promise I won't do it again.

Teachers and parents should teach children that honesty is the best policy. If you make a mistake, you should admit it so the punishment will be less severe.

We all know what is right and wrong. When we do the right thing, everybody likes us. When we make a mistake, we need to correct it.

"Please Put Your Cell Phone Away"

Objective

Teens often reach the age when parents allow them to have a cell phone. At that time, these devices become figuratively part of the student's body. They are either glued to an ear or stuck to the student's fingers. Students do not feel that they can put down their cell phones for fear that they will lose touch with reality. Unfortunately, cell phones and education don't mix. No matter how good a multitasker the student is, he or she simply cannot learn and text at the same time.

For safety reasons, students need their phones with them at all times. They do not, however, need to use them at all times. For this reason, it is absolutely essential that students turn off their phones while in class. Do they? Not if they want to stay in touch with the rest of the world.

Teachers are between a rock and hard place. Their first inclination is to collect the phones. This was tried in the school where I worked, but it didn't work because of the amount of time that was wasted. The best that can be expected is to have students turn their phones off and put them away. Some students do what they are told, while others will not be denied under any circumstances. The results are mixed with some trying to learn and others being more interested in keeping the lines of communication open.

The following script illustrates what happens when there are mixed attitudes toward cell phones in class:

Script

KELLY Jennifer, why are you crying, and why did you have to go to the principal's office?

JENNIFER The teacher said I'm going to be suspended.

KELLY What did you do?

JENNIFER I got out of my seat and punched Norman in the head.

KELLY Why did you do that? What did he do to you?

JENNIFER He sent me a text accusing me of being a slut.

KELLY You know he is an idiot. Why did you let it bother you?

JENNIFER I know he is, but he sent the message to five other people.

KELLY So, you had your phone on, you got out of your seat, and you punched an idiot in the head. Couldn't you think of any other rules to break?

JENNIFER I'm sure the teacher will think of some others. She was furious because I hit him in the middle of her lesson. The class went nuts, and the lesson was declared over by the teacher. She called the principal and had two students accompany me to the office.

KELLY   What happened to Norman?

JENNIFER   He got up to hit me back, but the teacher screamed and he stopped. When I left the room, he had a big red lump on his forehead. I really hit him hard. The teacher wants him suspended too. She said he insulted me by sending the message on his phone.

KELLY   What did the principal say?

JENNIFER   It went better than I thought. The principal saw that we hadn't been in trouble before and called our parents to pick us up from school today. He was more upset that we were using our phones in class than that we had had a fight. He reminded us that we were in school to learn and that the incident destroyed learning for that class. He also demanded that we apologize to the teacher and the class. He told us that if we were caught on our phones in class again, our parents would be instructed to keep them at home.

KELLY   That wasn't so bad. I thought you'd be suspended for sure. I wonder how our classmates feel about the incident.

Problems

Using phones while in class doesn't allow students to learn.
If students are on the phone, they are not paying attention.
Telephones can cause fights and other distractions.
Texting does not allow students to concentrate on what the teacher is saying.
If a teacher has to stop someone from using his or her phone, it interrupts the lesson.

Comments

- "Phones represent safety if there is an attack."
- "Phones that ring or vibrate are very annoying in class."
- "Phones keep us in touch with friends and relatives."
- "I hate it when a friend calls and wastes my time with unimportant stuff."
- "If I'm in class and my phone rings, I lose my train of thought."

Solutions

- Turn your phone off, not put it on vibrate, when entering class. It takes seconds to turn it on when needed.
- Switch your phone to vibrate while in class, in case your parents are trying to reach you.
- Teachers should collect all phones as students enter the room.
- Teachers should remove the phone from any student who is texting in class.

Sample Paragraphs

Using phones while in class doesn't allow students to learn. If students are on the phone, they are not paying attention. If a teacher has to stop someone from using his or her phone, it interrupts the lesson.

Phones represent safety if there is an attack. Phones keep teens in touch with friends and relatives. I hate it when a friend calls and wastes my time with unimportant stuff.

Turn your phone off, not put it on vibrate, when entering class. It takes seconds to turn it on when needed.

"Who Has the Money?"

Discussion

Yet another sensitive issue that affects many young teens is spending money. This lesson deals with a ninth grader who is invited to a sports event that can is expensive. He tries to bow out gracefully but is met by an insistent classmate who doesn't understand the problems that many inner-city children face. The script illustrates problems that are inherent in the inner city.

People lose jobs and may be without income for prolonged periods. Their children must adjust to the changes in the family situation and react accordingly. Those children who belong to fluid families don't know and are often unsympathetic to their classmates.

The idea that the rich get richer while the poor get poorer is a statement of fact. Even in a good economy, when both parents are working, and some working two jobs, there are times when families run short of money The children of those who are more fortunate often can't understand that some of their classmates may have less than they have.

Teachers must step in and explain that family situations may change and affect the spending habits of classmates. The following script will lay the groundwork for the teacher's job:

Script

STEVE   Hi, David. How are you?

DAVID   I'm fine. What's up?

STEVE   A bunch of guys are going to the football game this Sunday. My dad is going to drive us, and we want you to come with us.

DAVID   What do I need to do?

STEVE   You just have to pay for your seat. Sometimes my dad buys us a beer.

DAVID   Those tickets are a lot of money. I don't know if I can go.

STEVE   You have to come. Five of us are going, We are going to have a great time.

DAVID   I heard that the tickets can be as much as a hundred dollars. That's a lot of money.

STEVE   So what? We're going to have a great time, and if our team wins, they'll be in the playoffs.

DAVID   I would love to go, but I don't think my family can spare the money.

STEVE   You have to come. You are one of us.

DAVID   I don't know. My dad just started his new job, and we have been on a tight budget. I really can't ask him for that much money.

STEVE   You have to come. We all want you to be with us.

DAVID   I'll join you for something that costs less.

STEVE   Let's ask the other guys if they want you to join us.

Problems

Inner-city children may have money issues caused by low family incomes.

Children can be selfish and may not realize that others cannot do what they do.

Teachers may be insensitive to selfishness and jealousy among students.

Families are different and money may be limited in large families or parents may be between jobs.

Comments

- "David should ask his parents for the money so he can go to the football game."
- "Steve should understand that David can't spend his family's money when they are short on funds."
- "Steve should ask his friends to pay for his ticket."
- "Those who have more than others should share their good fortune."

Solutions

- David should ask his parents if they can afford to let him go to the game.
- Steve should drop his insistence that David join him and the others at the game. The other five students should chip in an extra twenty dollars each so that David can go to the game with them.
- The teacher should teach a lesson explaining that different families have various financial situations and that students should be sensitive to the situations of their classmates.

Sample Paragraphs

Inner-city children may have money issues caused by low family incomes. Sometimes children can be selfish and may not realize that others cannot do what they do. Steve should understand that David can't spend his family's money when they are short on funds.

Teachers must explain that families are different and that money may be limited in large families or that parents may be between jobs. The teacher should teach a lesson explaining that different families have various financial situations and that students should be sensitive to the situations of their classmates.

"What Do You Mean, I Didn't Make the Grade?"

Discussion

All teens are different. They mature at different rates, their learning ability varies, and they have different interests. Unfortunately, in most states public schools have a single curriculum, which means that students need to adapt to the curriculum rather than the curriculum being adapted to the student's needs. Young teens have their work cut out for them when they are interested in one area of academics but have to learn about ancient history or algebra. The results can be devastating.

My oldest granddaughter is a genius. She is in the fourth grade but is reading at the level of grade ten and scoring 100 percent on every math test. She scored in the ninety-ninth percentile in state tests. Her school has called in specialists to help her advance, but she is bored with school. On the other hand, some students are either uninterested in or unable to excel in many school subjects that they consider unimportant.

Boredom or a disinterest in subjects that do not interest certain students can result in their failure in these subjects. The following script illustrates a student who is earning As in all subjects except history, where her grade is a D. The student has no interest in what happened two thousand years ago or in how our nation was formed. Does this mean that this student will not be a successful member of society?

Script

JANICE   I can't believe I failed the history test again. I tried to study, but nothing went in.

EMILY   History is easy. What is giving you so much trouble?

JANICE   I don't know. I read the books, but it doesn't seem to sink in.

EMILY   Why don't we study together for the next test? I can ask you questions that we might see on the test, and we can discuss what we are reading.

JANICE   I don't know if that will work. I draw a mental block every time I open the book.

EMILY   Maybe you should ask your parents to get you a tutor. A tutor might be able to get through your block.

JANICE   I really don't want involve them. They think I am earning all As and would be very disappointed to learn I'm screwing up.

EMILY   They'll be more upset if you fail and don't tell them. Think of what it will do to your transcript for getting into colleges.

STEPHEN ABRAMOWITZ

JANICE You're right. I'll talk to the teacher tomorrow. I'll do whatever she recommends to help me get out of this funk.

EMILY You should also talk to our classmates. Maybe they'll have suggestions to help.

Problems

Janice is a good student. She does well in all subjects except history. If students have no use for certain subjects, they shouldn't be forced to learn them.

Students should be tested so that they know what they are suited for.

Curricula should be reevaluated to make subjects more interesting to students and revised so that students aren't required to take subjects they don't like or need.

Comments

- "All students have favorite subjects. They should not be punished if they don't do well in all subjects."
- "Students should be tested to see where their interests are. These tests should be aimed at their strengths, so they can become experts in their respective fields."
- "Curricula should be changed so that they become more interesting to students."
- "Curricula should be changed so that they are relevant to jobs and student interests."

Solutions

- Change the curriculum so that it is more interesting and more relevant to students.
- Test students to see where their interests lie.
- Make sure that curricula encourage students to pursue interests in their favorite areas.
- Teachers should encourage students to pursue their interests.

Sample Paragraph

If students have no use for certain subjects, then why are they forced to learn them? Students should be tested so that they know what they are suited for. Curricula should be reevaluated to make subjects more interesting to students. All students have favorite subjects. They should not be punished if they don't do well in all subjects. Curricula should be changed so that they become more interesting to students and are relevant to jobs and student interests. Students should be tested to see where their interests lie, and teachers should encourage students to pursue those interests.

"I Hate My Parents"

Discussion

In today's world, both parents are often forced to work in order to support the family. In single-parent families, the parent is sometimes required to take two jobs. This puts a great strain on other family members, who are often called on to take several jobs of their own. Most families rally around the parents where possible, and the younger children need help and guidance to grow into productive adults. In many cases grandparents (in China, grandparents almost always raise children while both parents work), aunts, and nannies serve as surrogate parents, helping to raise younger children. In many cases, however, the job of raising young children falls on the shoulders of older siblings. Teens are often required to take younger siblings to school, walk them home, and babysit for them until parents get home from work.

Unfortunately, parents are often tired, hungry, and unable to deal with their young children after a long day at work. Despite this, young children still need to do homework and be fed, bathed, and cared for until they fall asleep. If a parent works late hours or shirks his or her (or their) responsibility, the task often falls on the shoulders of the older sibling. All too often, this leads to resentment because the older sibling, in addition to having to be responsible for himself or herself, also has to be responsible for a younger child. This resentment can build as the younger sibling becomes needier and requires more attention. In some cases, this resentment can turn into animosity toward both the younger child and the parent(s).

In the following script, one such teen discusses this problem with a friend who does not have the same responsibilities:

Script

TAMARA   Why did you fall asleep in class today?

MADISON   I was exhausted and couldn't keep my eyes open.

TAMARA   What happened to make you so tired?

MADISON   Nothing unusual. I had to take care of my younger brother and couldn't do my homework until he fell asleep.

TAMARA   Where were your parents?

MADISON   They both work until eight o'clock and are tired and hungry when they get home.

TAMARA   But he is their son, so they should take care of him.

MADISON   Again, they get home at eight o'clock and claim that they are too tired, so I have to help him with his dinner, homework, and his bath. They kiss him good night, but if he can't fall asleep, they ask me to sit with him.

TAMARA   But that's not fair.

MADISON   Tell me about it. This has gone on for months. They claim I have to do my share for the family. When he finally falls asleep, I have to do my homework, bathe, and get myself ready for bed. I hate that I have to take care of my brother, and I hate my parents for making me take care of him.

TAMARA   I can see why. If my parents made me take care of my little sister, I would be pissed too. Luckily, my mom doesn't work, so she picks my sister up from school, and I am free to do as I like.

MADISON   The worst part is that I can't go out or to a friend's house. They also discourage me from spending a long time on the phone. Thank heavens my dad goes shopping for food, or they would have me doing that too.

TAMARA   What can you do to change the situation?

MADISON   Not much. I'll be doing this until my brother can take care of himself. Even then I'll probably have to help with his homework.

TAMARA   I wonder how many of our classmates also have to deal with their younger siblings? Maybe we should ask them.

Problems

Madison fell asleep in class.

Both of Madison's parents have to work late to support the family.

Madison is responsible for helping her brother with his homework, feeding him, bathing him, and getting him ready for bed.

Madison cannot take care of her own needs until after her brother goes to sleep.

Madison stays up late getting her work done.

Comments

- "It is unfair to make Madison take care of her brother."
- "I help with my siblings, but I am not the only one who takes care of them."
- "Madison's parents should hire someone to help take care of her brother."
- "Maybe one of Madison's parents should change their work hours so they could be home to help."
- "It is not fair to Madison to make her take care of her brother. She should have time to take care of herself and socialize with her friends."
- "Madison should be paid for taking care of her brother."

Solutions

- One of Madison's parents should change work hours so that he or she can be home to help.
- Madison should take her brother to a friend's or relative's house after school so that she has help with her brother.
- Madison's parents should hire a nanny or babysitter to help Madison with her brother.

Sample Paragraph

Madison fell asleep in class. Both of Madison's parents have to work late to support the family. Madison is responsible for helping her brother with his homework, feeding him, bathing him, and getting him ready for bed. Madison cannot take care of her own needs until after her brother goes to sleep. She stays up late getting her work done. It is unfair to make Madison take care of her brother. Maybe one of Madison's parents should change their work hours so they could be home to help. Or they should hire a nanny or babysitter to help their daughter with her brother. And finally, Madison should be paid for taking care of her brother.

"I'm Running for Class President"

Discussion

One of the problems young teens face is acceptance. As they grow, they struggle to find their place in society. Actually, they need to find their place in societies. A young teen must fight for acceptance among the adults whom he or she considers important and in peer societies, which affect his or her everyday existence. Adult societies include parents and their friends, the teen's teachers, religious leaders, and those who keep the teen well (doctors, nurses, psychologists, and others). Peer societies include classmates, sports team members, friends, and possible romantic contacts. These relationships are extremely important to a young teen at this time of life.

Those who cannot successfully establish successful interactions experience anxiety and insecurity. In fact, those young teens who fail to be accepted and feel as if they cannot be comfortable in relationships may suffer from depression, feelings of disconnection, and bouts of isolationism. Media pressure can make them feel even more confused, defiant, and out of control. Most important is the feeling of not belonging to society. This issue can affect all aspects of a young teen's life.

In the following script, there is student new to the school. This student is in dire need of being accepted into the school's society. To enable this to happen, he has decided to run for class president. No one knows him, and his classmates wonder why he has chosen to run. He promises to be their leader, to make everyone's life better, and to be their representative with all teachers, even though he has no relationship with any of the educators. He does not consider the consequences of losing the election or the damage a loss would mean to his being accepted by his peers.

Script

SUSAN   Hi! Welcome to our class. What's your name?

JOSEPH   My name is Joseph. I heard someone call you Susan.

SUSAN   That's me. Where are you from, Joseph?

JOSEPH   I'm from the Midwest. Chicago to be exact. Ever been there?

SUSAN   Nope. Born and bred here in Miami. What brings you to our fair city?

JOSEPH   My parents split. My mom has relatives down here, so here I am. You have a great school and a great class. I am going to like it here.

SUSAN   Well, I'm glad you like us. That will help you to blend in.

JOSEPH   I'm sure I will. I heard your class is having an election for class president next week. I am planning to run.

SUSAN   You're kidding, right? You don't know anyone, and they surely know nothing about you. Besides, John is running, and everyone likes him. What do you hope to gain?

JOSEPH   l hope to become the leader of the class. If not, I'll at least make a lot of friends. I did the same thing in Chicago, and I won.

SUSAN   First of all, you're not in Chicago. Second, down here you have to earn your friends, and that can't be done in one week. Third, the teachers won't like you unless you earn their trust and respect.

JOSEPH   You'd be amazed at how their attitudes will change if I am elected. I'll become the star of the class, and our teachers will treat me like a superstar. I'll become a king, and I'll be accepted by everyone.

SUSAN   So, that's what this is about—your need to be accepted into our school. Your plan won't work. Many of us have been together for years. A stranger can't become a star in one week.

JOSEPH   l have nothing to lose. It worked once before. Besides, I saw a TV show that claimed that most teenagers look for a leader. It showed that by being aggressive, you can get ahead.

SUSAN   If you are going to believe TV shows, you'll be an ax murderer next month If you were smart, you'd start talking to our classmates. The more friends you make, the better your chances.

JOSEPH   l plan to do that. Can I count on your vote?

SUSAN   l can't promise you anything. John and I have been friends since first grade. I owe him loyalty, which he has earned. Talk to the other students.

Problems

Joseph, a newly arrived student, plans to run for president of the class one week before the election.

Joseph did this once before, in his hometown, and won the election. This made him popular with his fellow students and with teachers. He gained acceptance at his school.

Joseph is running against a student who has yearslong established friendships at the school.

Susan doesn't think Joseph has a chance to win the election. She recognizes Joseph's need to be accepted but cautions him that he's moving too fast because relationships are built on trust and mutual respect.

Comments

- "John has been a friend of the students at that school for many years. He is accepted as a leader and deserves to be class president."
- "Joseph is trying to become a superstar in one week. Many students won't vote for him until they know him better."

Solutions

- Joseph needs to withdraw from the election until he establishes himself as a respected member of the school.
- John needs to step up his campaign in order to win the election.
- Joseph needs to get counseling to deal with problem of needing to be accepted.
- Students of Susan's class need to determine who deserves their vote for president.

Sample Paragraph

Joseph, a newly arrived student, plans to run for president of the class one week before the election. He is running against a student who has yearslong established friendships at the school. Joseph did this once before, in his hometown, and won the election. This made him popular with his fellow students and with teachers. He gained acceptance in his school. Now Joseph is trying to become a superstar in one week. But most students won't vote for him until they know him better. Joseph needs to withdraw from the election until he establishes himself as a respected member of the school. Students of Susan's class need to determine who deserves their vote for president.

"But Cousin Brian Said It Was All Right"

Discussion

Young adults are children turning into adults. They can be molded by parents, relatives, teachers, and peers. One of the most important skills a young teen must learn is to make adult decisions about things that will affect him or her for a long time to come. Teens are often pressured to do things the way others do them. Of course, very few people will ever admit that what they do is wrong. They've either learned to deny any wrongdoing by watching their parents, seeing people in the media deflect blame, or worst of all, trying it themselves and seeing it work. I can't remember the last time anybody told me that what they do is wrong. Therefore, if this tactic of denial has worked for so many, then young teens should do things the same way. Unfortunately, teens have no experience with adult situations and must look to others for advice.

As an example, according to the National Institute on Alcohol Abuse, 14.1 million adults suffer from alcohol use disorder. Talbot Recovery claims that 60 percent of men drink regularly. What kind of example does this set for teens? What advice would these men offer to teens who are considering drinking alcohol as a way to relax or escape?

Parents set high standards for their teens. They expect their children to have a better life than they had by getting good grades in school. Additionally, they expect their teens to have great friends, participate in extracurricular activities, and be responsible family members.

Peers expect teens to become popular among their equals. They expect all students to conform to general rules set by the majority, also expecting that each other be cooperative, have an active social life, and participate in group activities.

The combination of family members and schoolmates applies pressure to mold an adolescent into what all these individuals expect them to be. Pressure being applied from several sources pulls a naive teen in different directions. If a teen does not know who is right or does not make decisions for himself or herself, the result can be frustration and depression.

In the following script, we find two students discussing the pressures exerted on them by various sources:

Script

Lois Hey, Sam, how's it going?

Sam It's not. I am on lockdown for the next two weeks.

Lois Wow. What did you do?

Sam I went to the movies with my cousin Brian.

Lois Why would that get you grounded for two weeks?

SAM   My parents didn't know where I was. My cousin called and said there were two great science-fiction movies in town and asked if I wanted to go with him. It was Saturday, and he said we could see both movies. He said my parents wouldn't mind and that he had his parents' car.

LOIS   What went wrong?

SAM   The first movie was scheduled to begin in a few minutes, and we had to hurry. I told him I would have to call my parents, but he assured me that they wouldn't mind if I was with him. He told me he would lend me the money for the tickets, saying I could pay him back when I got my allowance. My parents were not home, but again, Brian said it would be OK if I went with him.

LOIS   Didn't your parents try to reach you when they saw you weren't home?

SAM   Yes, but when I entered the theater, we had to turn our phones off. When the first movie ended, we had to rush to the second theater, and we forgot to turn our phones on.

LOIS   So, your parents didn't know where you were until you got home? No wonder you got grounded for two weeks. I would have done the same. What happened to your cousin?

SAM   My mother called his mother, and he was grounded for two weeks too.

LOIS   I wonder if other friends or classmates have been grounded and why. I think we should ask.

Problems

Sam listened to his cousin and made a bad decision.

Sam and his cousin went to the movies without telling their parents. They turned off their phones in the theater, so their parents couldn't reach them.

They went to a second movie but did not turn on their phones. Sam's parents were very angry and grounded Sam for two weeks. His cousin was also grounded.

Comments

- "Students admit to having sleepovers, going to malls, and visiting friends without telling their parents."
- "In today's world, it is necessary that parents know where their children are at all times."

Solutions

- Sam should not have gone with his cousin unless his parents knew where he was going. He should have turned on his phone while they walked between theaters.
- Sam should have left his parents a note before he left home.
- Sam's parents should have called around to try find out where Sam may have gone. When Brian's parents didn't know where their son was either, they could have guessed the boys were together.

Sample Paragraph

   Sam listened to his cousin and made a bad decision. Sam and his cousin went to the movies without telling their parents. They turned off their phones in the theater, so their parents couldn't reach them. They went to a second movie but did not turn on their phones. In today's world, it is necessary that parents know where their children are at all times. Students admit to having sleepovers, going to malls, and visiting friends without telling their parents. Sam should not have gone with his cousin unless his parents knew where he was going. He should have left his parents a note before he left home.

"I'm Rich"

Discussion

The morals of the United States have changed. People used to act for the greater good of all. Today, however, we see movements that focus on individual personal needs. We have reduced these needs to a simple thought: *It's all about me.* Most everyone is interested only in what they can gain for themselves. These attitudes start in the home and continue in our schools. Unsuspecting teens are indoctrinated into thinking that they are more important than anyone else. They therefore develop hedonistic behaviors and lifestyles.

A Gallop poll conducted in May 2018 shows that 50 percent of Americans believed that the state of moral values in the United States was "poor." Another 37 percent of adults said that moral values were "fair." Only 14 percent of Americans felt that moral values were "good." With the country in turmoil in recent years, one can only assume that things have gotten worse.

Our teens are facing pressures from all sides. Edward Gibbons identifies three major causes of poor behavior among teens: (1) the breakdown of the family, (2) a strong craving for pleasure, and (3) loss of religion. In this lesson, we deal with a young teen who found a wallet with cash, credit cards, and identification. He is thrilled, with a belief in the adage "finders keepers (losers weepers)." The three causes just listed give our young teen the impetus to spend the cash and use the wallet for his own gain. He has no guilt and does not feel it necessary to discuss his find with his family. Instead, he turns to a friend who he feels shares his joy. Without going into the many arguments about why keeping the wallet is an immoral choice, we will investigate the effects of a moral friend on our morally deficient teen.

Script

SAUL   I'm rich!

JEROME   What do you mean?

SAUL   l found this wallet on the street. It has a hundred dollars in cash and lots of credit cards.

JEROME   What do you plan to do with it?

SAUL   Are you kidding? I plan on buying video games and hiding in my room for weeks playing them.

JEROME   Do you think that is the right thing to do?

SAUL   Why not?

JEROME   Because the money isn't yours. Don't you feel guilty about stealing someone else's money?

SAUL It's not stealing. She lost it and I found it. What would you do with the money?

JEROME You have her name and address. I would return the money and wallet. What if the owner needs the money? She may have a family who needs that cash. My aunt lost her wallet, and it took weeks for her to cancel her credit cards and get new ones. She couldn't buy anything for the family until all her cards were replaced. She also lost a lot of cash, which also hurt her family. But the real deal rests with you. You know what the right thing to do is. Think of how you'll feel knowing that you did wrong or how you'll you feel knowing that you took something that doesn't belong to you. Think of the trouble you will get into if you try to use her credit cards.

SAUL Why would I get into trouble?

JEROME You will be a teenage male using a card with a woman's name on it. No cashier will give you merchandise without calling the police.

SAUL I didn't know that. Maybe you're right and I should return the wallet. The woman lives near our school. Would you come with me to return the wallet?

JEROME If you want me to, I'll go with you. I'll tell my parents that I'll be late coming home from school. I know you're doing the right thing and that you'll feel great by returning the wallet.

(One day later.)

SAUL I feel I did the right thing. The woman could not stop thanking me for returning her wallet. I couldn't believe that she told me to keep the hundred dollars as a reward for returning it. My parents told me that they were very proud of me for doing the right thing. Thank you for convincing me to do the right thing and for coming with me. I am going to use the reward money to buy video games. Do you want one?

JEROME No. You did the right thing, so you deserve the reward. I'm glad that you did what was right. I'm also happy that your parents are proud of you. When you set up the games, I'd like to come over and play them with you.

SAUL You've got it. I wonder what our classmates would have done in my situation.

JEROME I think we should ask them. I also think we should tell our teacher and ask her to talk about the moral decision you made.

Problems

The morals of our country are changing, and most people are out to make things better for themselves. Saul found a wallet with cash and credit cards. He wants to keep the wallet and use the cash to buy video games.

The woman who lost her wallet faced weeks of getting her cards renewed and couldn't buy anything until she got new ones.

Comments

- "Saul did the right thing by returning the wallet to the woman."
- "Saul made his parents proud that he did the right thing."
- "I would have kept the wallet and bought lots of stuff."
- "Saul should not have thought about keeping the wallet."

Solutions

Teachers and parents must teach their children right from wrong. They must establish norms that students are required to adopt, treating others in the way that they would want to be treated themselves. Teachers and parents must also teach students that they are members of several societies and that they must do what is right to benefit all members of these societies.

Sample Paragraphs

Saul found a wallet with cash and credit cards. He wanted to keep the wallet and buy video games. The woman who lost her wallet faced weeks of getting her cards renewed and couldn't buy anything until she got new ones. Saul should not have thought about keeping the wallet. But he did the right thing by returning the wallet to the woman.

Teachers and parents must teach their children right from wrong. They must establish norms that students are required to follow, treating others in the way that they would want to be treated themselves.

"Does It Ever End?"

Objective

After a recent discussion about the state of affairs in the world, I commented that I feel really bad for the future of my grandchildren. Young teens are facing more challenges than ever before, and situations seem to get worse every day. *Teen Problems and How Adults Can Help Solve Them* is dedicated to solving problems that young teens may face in their daily relationships. They need to take control of themselves when dealing with the problems they face from day to day. Unfortunately, there are some problems that young teens cannot solve by themselves. In virtually every area of the country, populations are affected by tragedies, some of which are caused by weather, some of which are caused by disease, some of which are caused by health crises, some of which may be caused by inherited deficiencies, and some of which may be caused by political interactions between areas of the world. These outside influences may be just as damaging to a young teen as personal conflicts.

According to the Johns Hopkins Center for Adolescent Health, teens are dealing with many challenges for the first time, which makes them more vulnerable than adults, who have experienced a variety of trials during their lifetimes. Adolescents have different developmental needs compared to older people. Young teens are in the process of separating from their parents while developing social connections through interactions with peers. Some process situations emotionally, while others are more logic oriented, the processing style being influenced by the type of challenge the teen faces. In all tragedies, the most effective help comes from one source: parents. (With regard to an epidemic, parents must stress that the virus is not likely to make children sick because most of them do not have underlying conditions but that they must keep others safe.)

When tragedies occur, young teens lose one of the most important values they possess: their identity. Teenagers need to establish themselves with their peers and other members of society. Tragedies that prohibit them from going to school or mixing with other members of their society are devastating to their physical and psychological well-being. The inability to participate in sports combined with the lack of socialization can halt both kinds of growth. These situations accentuate the common problems that teens face every day. With a lack of contact with people, teens cannot identify with communities beyond their families. (They don't have access to mentors, role models, and heroes.) They stress about not having the tools to manage their time. They are only subject to their parents' expectations, which may not match those of peers and society in general. All these things can have devastating effects, resulting in mental and physical health problems, drug and alcohol abuse, unhealthy social media use, online bullying, and risky sexual behavior.

Books have been written about teens who have been damaged by personal tragedies. The following online conversation will serve to highlight some of the problems:

Script

Tracey   Hi, Samantha. It's been awhile. How are you?

Samantha   I don't want to ruin your day, but I am a mess. As you know, a tornado ripped off the roof on my house and we had to move to my grandparents' house in another state. Then my dad got a job, and we moved to yet another state. This state has schools locked down, and I am learning on Zoom. I hate looking at tiny squares on my computer, and I get headaches, so I have to rest my eyes every few minutes. This makes it difficult to concentrate, so I am not doing well with my classes. I feel like I have lost a year and a half at a time when I should be growing. Because I don't get much exercise, I put on ten pounds and I feel like a blimp. This has me depressed. My friend John has stopped corresponding with me, so I lost a good friend. My parents work from home and are on my back constantly. I have no contact with anyone, and I feel like I'm in jail. But enough about my misery. How are you doing, Samantha?

Samantha   Well, since I saw you last, my boobs have grown substantially, and every time I go on Zoom, I feel like a porn star.

Tracey   I'll bet you're getting more attention from the boys in your class.

Samantha   I sure am. Unfortunately, it is the wrong kind of attention. The only saving grace is that I don't have to be with them every day. In fact, since the virus took center stage, I am not with anyone most days. My parents are driving me crazy though. I am depressed about being isolated and not being able to live life as we knew it.

Tracey   Samantha, you won't do anything stupid, will you?

Samantha   No, even though three students in our school offed themselves. I keep telling myself that things will go back to being normal.

Tracey   I feel the same way. I keep hearing about rising suicide rates, and I convince myself that things will get better.

Samantha   I miss you. Is there any chance you can home for a visit?

Tracey   Home? I don't know where home is. I'm not even sure who I am anymore. Last week we ate outside at a restaurant for the first time. I felt like we were breaking the law. We had to sit away from others, and we had to wear masks until they brought the food. Then we went home to lock ourselves away from the rest of the world.

Samantha   Tell me about it. I haven't seen anyone in almost a year. I'm tired of being locked up with my parents, and I hope to see other family members before I'm old.

Tracey   I feel the same way. Let's get online and see what our friends have to say.

Problems

Tragedies greatly affect the lives of young teens. They are not old enough to deal with the major changes that occur in their lives and are ill-equipped to deal with life's disruptions.

Teens who are affected by tragedies lose their social identity and physical skills.

Young teens who survive tragedies are dominated by their parents and often can't handle the relationship. They have no one to turn to.

Teens cannot connect with society when they are being uprooted by moves and isolation.

Young teens who have experienced tragedies usually do not have access to mentors, role models, or heroes.

Young teens have additional responsibilities that put further strain on their time. Parents often use their teens to supervise younger siblings and assume more household responsibilities.

The rates of depression and suicide among teens after a tragedy are higher than ever before.

Tragedies that depress young teens cause them to look to drugs and alcohol to help them feel better.

Students who were educated online did not progress in their studies as much as they should have.

Comments

- "When Hurricane Sandy flooded my house several years ago, we were forced to move to an apartment in another area of New York City. I was forced to go to a different school for six months, and switching schools not only took me away from my friends but also negatively affected the way I learned."
- "My friend gained a lot of weight because she was scared."
- "My friend got so depressed that he needed to get help from a shrink."
- "My aunt's house was burned in a California wildfire. My cousins had to move to another state to live with relatives. They both dropped out of school and went to work."
- "My friend lost her father to COVID. She became so emotional that she needed to spend time in a mental hospital. A year later she committed suicide."
- "My friend started using drugs after admitting that he was miserable after a mudslide buried his home."

Solutions

- Teens must be taught about the kinds of tragedies that might affect their lives.
- Parents are their most important lifeline and must prepare their children for many types of situations.
- Parents must also be their teen's support team if an adverse situation occurs. Families must come together as a unit to help each other deal with adverse situations.

- Schools must do their job in helping traumatized young teens. They should set up suicide prevention classes for students who are in danger.
- Teachers must be taught to look for signs of depression and pain in students and refer them for help if needed.
- Groups or clubs must be formed to allow young teens to socialize and attend purposeful events to help them reintegrate into society.
- Antidrug and anti-alcohol-abuse classes should be formed to help teens avoid seeking escape through use of these substances.

Sample Paragraph

Tragedies greatly affect the lives of teens, who are not old enough to deal with the major changes that occur in their lives and are ill-equipped to deal with life's disruptions. Young teens who have experienced tragedies usually do not have access to mentors, role models, or heroes. The rates for depression and suicide among young teens after a tragedy are higher than ever before. Students who were educated online did not progress in their studies as much as they should have. When Hurricane Sandy flooded my house several years ago, we were forced to move to an apartment in another area of New York City. I was forced to go to a different school for six months, and switching schools not only took me away from my friends, but also negatively affected the way I learn. Young teens must be taught about the kinds of tragedies that might affect their lives. Parents are their most important lifeline and must prepare their children for many types of situations. Schools must do their job in helping traumatized teens. They should set up suicide prevention classes for students who are in danger.

"I Can't Believe He's Gone"

Objective

Teens face a great amount of pressure. Their main job is to do well in school, but their responsibilities at home increase tremendously in high school. They need to learn and make use of time management skills to handle the extra workload. They need to deal with problems that arise when they go through puberty. They face physical health issues. They also face violence in the form of bullying, both in-person and online. They must adapt to tragedies that affect their lives. Many teens cannot deal with the constant challenge. This entire book is devoted to the problems young teens face as they mature. I have covered the problems comprehensively.

One must consider alternatives that teens may choose to escape from the pressures that drain them. Unfortunately, a major form of escape that is enticing to teens is the use of drugs and alcohol. And why not? Adults use these substances to escape their problems, and parents would be hypocritical to forbid their teens from doing the same. Alcohol is readily available most everywhere and is often unsecured in most homes, allowing teens access without penalty. The drug situation has changed drastically over the past several years. Marijuana and cocaine have infiltrated our country from South American countries. So much pot has become available in this country that many states have voted to legalize it in order to create income. In fact, the federal government is considering making it a national product to compete with the mass amount of drugs pouring in across our borders and to get its share of the income from the sales. At this point, however, the majority of drugs available to Americans are illegal. This means that the people using street drugs are possibly buying drugs that are laced with other substances. A major killer that can be found in both marijuana and cocaine is fentanyl. Opioids used for pain reduction have also been found both by prescription and on the open market. (Both fentanyl and other opioids can slow down or stop a person's breathing, causing death by overdose.)

No one can be sure of what they are buying when purchasing foreign substances, and therefore people are putting themselves in great danger when they use these drugs. According to the National Institute for Drug Abuse, since 2018, teen overdoses have increased.

The following script is a true story illustrating the tragedy of drug abuse and the effects on those around the drug abuser:

Script

JORDAN   Hey, Logan, I am so sorry about your loss. Nick and I played basketball together on the school team. All of us on the team are devastated.

LOGAN   Thanks, Jordan. It hasn't hit me yet. I expect to get home and find my brother in his room. I will be lost without him. He was my hero and the most important influence in my life since I was a baby.

JORDAN   I feel the same way about my brother. I can't imagine losing him. Your parents must be suffering terribly. I'm sorry, I shouldn't be asking you to talk about your loss.

LOGAN   It's OK. Talking about it will help me deal with reality. My parents are drinking themselves to sleep. Yesterday they started taking Nick's room apart. They threw his bed in the garbage and packed his books to return to the school. He has actually been in trouble for two years. He joined the wrong crowd and started experimenting with drugs. When my parents realized he was getting stoned every day, they pulled him out of school and got him private tutoring. I thought it was working until recently. On Memorial Day, my parents left the house to meet some friends for dinner. As soon as they left, Nick left to meet with his friends, his old crowd, and got stoned again. The drugs he took must have been laced with opioids, maybe fentanyl, because he looked awful when he got home. I asked if he wanted to watch TV with me, but he told me he was going to bed. When my mother went to wake him the next morning, she saw he wasn't breathing. She called an ambulance, but it was too late. The EMTs called the coroner, who took my brother away in a van. The next day the coroner came to the house and told us Nick had died of a drug overdose, but it would take weeks to get the forensics report. The police came later and asked my parents if they knew where my brother had gotten the drugs that killed him. They gave them the names of the friends he used to hang out with, and they left. We've been crying for days.

JORDAN   I am sorry I made you tell me the story.

LOGAN   Don't be sorry. I actually feel better. You're the first person I've opened up to. I'm glad you're my friend.

JORDAN   Please let me know if there is anything I can do to help. Anytime you need someone to talk to, I'll be there. I'm wondering what our friends have to say about your story. Let's ask them if they have heard similar stories.

Problems

Pressure on teens can cause them to seek relief from drugs and alcohol.

Unfortunately, illegal drugs are sometimes laced with additional drugs that can cause death. When a teen overdoses, his or her family suffers terribly.

Tragedies increase the number of overdoses by reducing a teen's ability to cope with the situation.

Comments

- "Tragedies have changed teens' attitudes toward the use of drugs and alcohol."
- "My brother broke his arm and was given pills for the pain. He kept going back to the doctor for more pills. My parents finally sent him for help."

- "My cousin smoked a joint and got very sick. He was in the hospital for two days."
- "Students have to be aware of the dangers of drug use when drugs are laced with other drugs that can kill them."
- "Parents and teachers must become aware of changes in their children and get them help if they feel they are taking drugs."

Solutions

- Teens must be desensitized to the negative effects of life challenges. Parents are the most important resource to help their teens stay mentally healthy and away from drugs and alcohol.
- Teachers, parents, relatives, coaches, clergy, et al. all have an obligation to notice and report changes in teens' attitudes, habits, health, learning abilities, and social relationships.
- Schools must play a greater role in ensuring diagnosis and treatment of teens who may be in danger of escaping through the use drugs and/or alcohol.

Sample Paragraphs

Pressures on teens can cause them to seek relief in drugs and alcohol. Unfortunately, illegal drugs are sometimes laced with additional drugs that can cause death. When a teen overdoses, his or her family suffers terribly. Students have to be aware of the dangers of drug use when drugs are laced with other drugs that can kill them. Parents are the most important resource to help their teens stay mentally healthy and away from drugs and alcohol.

Teachers, parents, relatives, coaches, clergy, et al. all have an obligation to notice and report changes in teens' attitudes, habits, health, learning abilities, and social relationships. Schools must play a greater role in ensuring diagnosis and treatment of teens who may be in danger of escaping through the use of drugs and/or alcohol.

"Don't Shoot!"

Objective

In recent years there has been a large increase in the number of teen crises. This trend is being fed by a number of circumstances. Lockdowns during the COVID-19 pandemic kept students out of school, canceled their socialization, and made them afraid of getting sick or watching loved ones (or even themselves) suffering from disease. Natural disasters and deteriorating family situations add to the problems facing young teens. (This whole book is designed to illustrate situations that force young teens to make decisions that can bring upon them unwanted circumstances.) Suddenly, they consider friends competitors, or even enemies, who are vying for the limited attention available in a disease-restricted world. When teens can't interact with those who think the way they do and have to take orders from those in authority who are more concerned with restricting their freedom than encouraging their growth, they become fearful. Not knowing what the future holds for them is another source of fear and pressure. Suicide for girls ages twelve to seventeen went up by 51 percent from February 2021 to March 2021. The result is that we must tech self-preservation at any cost.

This problem is exacerbated by a proliferation of firearms. An increase in crime has caused Americans to arm themselves for protection. The Second Amendment allows noncriminals to possess guns, although individual states have different rules about their use. Unfortunately, many states have liberal gun laws, so virtually anyone can obtain a firearm if they want one. In addition, adults who obtain weapons do not secure them properly, so sometimes teens have access to them. The results are young teens going on shooting sprees targeting fellow students and teachers in their school. And why not? Prosecution has changed and penalties for gun usage and gun crimes are being downgraded to the point of absolving anyone guilty of any gun crime short of murder.

Unfortunately, the problem of mass slayings is not restricted to schools. Young teens who have access to guns are taking their battles to the streets. Gangs seek revenge against competitors, and any teen with a grudge can seek revenge by shooting those who oppose them. Young teen students have to worry about the problem of gun violence every time they enter a school. The following script emphasizes the fear that young teens face:

Script

AVA   I am glad to be back in school after our vacation.

OWEN   Me too. I had a great summer, and I hope our school year goes well.

AVA   I'm concerned about all the violence that has been going on in all the schools. There are more shootings and bullying than ever before.

Owen I know, but I think that COVID is to blame. I know that I have become super angry over school policies and the lack of ability to confront problems because we are not in contact with those who have grudges and anger.

Ava I think that is a big factor in having everyone on edge, but I blame parents for allowing their children access to guns without explaining the consequences of gun crimes.

Owen I agree. I am also concerned about the rules our teachers are imposing on us with regard to keeping doors locked and hiding under our desks in an emergency. I feel like we are always in danger, and that affects the way we learn.

Ava True that. My parents talk to me every day about my feelings and events that effect my life. More than once they have asked if I needed to get help from a health professional. Unfortunately, very few of my classmates have similar conversations and are left to solve problems on their own. Their unguided solutions can lead to bullying and/or violence that can hurt others.

Owen I agree. That is why we have to be careful to keep our friends with us. We should definitely discuss this further.

Problems

Young teens need to be concerned about bullying and gun violence when they go to school.

Guns are too available to parents and their children, and better control requirements are needed to keep guns out of students' hands.

Parents must secure weapons and make sure that their children do not have access to any weapon.

Parents have to be more vigilant with their teens and need to talk to them daily to alleviate problems when they arise.

Teachers need to reduce bullying and be sensitive to students who seem troubled.

Health professionals need to be present to defuse situations that might lead to bullying or violence.

Schools should have more security to deter students from becoming belligerent.

Comments

- "Young teens are nervous every time they enter their school."
- "It takes the police a long time to respond to the school if there is a problem."
- "Parents need to make sure all weapons are secured and kept away from children."
- "Acts of violence are often preceded by bullying."
- "Steps must be taken to lessen this problem."
- "Students who commit violence must understand the ramifications when they are caught."

Solutions

- Gun laws must be strengthened to take guns out of the hands of those who should not have them.
- Ghost guns must be outlawed, and states must enforce laws to prevent guns from crossing their borders.
- Schools must have more security to protect their students from attack.
- Schools must have drills so that students know what to do in the event of an attack.
- Teachers, parents, and guidance counselors must identify at-risk students and get them help before there is an incident.
- All middle schools and high schools must install metal detectors to stop weapons from coming into the building.
- Students must be enlisted to identify friends who are having problems and might become problems in the future.
- Classes must be established to curb bullying and show how bullying can lead to violence.
- Students must be encouraged to travel with friends, which can lessen bullying and violence.

Final Thoughts

Our young teens are facing many problems as they grow into our next generation of leaders. They must deal with pressures from world conflicts, pressures from parental guidance, pressures from peers, and most importantly, pressures arising from their own physical maturation process. It is amazing that young teens can grow into healthy, productive members of society.

The scripts that you just read represent a small sample of the problems that our teens face in their day-to-day attempt to grow into healthy, well-functioning adults. Please consider these problems as a beginning to the exploration of the types of things that American teens experience in their attempts to become our future leaders.

About the Author

Stephen Abramowitz was an educator for the New York City Board of Education for more than thirty-five years—a teacher, a vice principal, and the director of a substance abuse prevention program. He worked with inner-city children and their siblings and parents. He served as a consultant for a drug prevention program at Rutgers University.

Mr. Abramowitz earned three master's degrees in different fields of education. While heading the drug prevention program, he wrote a curriculum to make young children aware of dangerous drugs and substances found in the home.

Printed in the United States
by Baker & Taylor Publisher Services